Nel Macdonald

A Concise Guide to
DOG
BREEDS

A CONCISE GUIDE TO
DOG
BREEDS

BRYAN RICHARD

Bath · New York · Singapore · Hong Kong · Cologne · Delhi · Melbourne

This edition published by
Parragon in 2010

Parragon
Queen Street House
4 Queen Street
Bath, BA1 1HE

Produced by Atlantic Publishing

For details of photograph copyrights see page 256
Text © Parragon Books Ltd 2006

ISBN 978-1-4054-7332-3
Printed in China

CONTENTS

WORKING BREEDS

SPORTING/GUNDOGS

HOUNDS

TERRIERS, PINSCHERS AND SCHNAUZERS

TOY AND COMPANION BREEDS

INTRODUCTION

This book is divided into the following sections: Herding Breeds, Working Breeds, Sporting and Gundog Breeds, Hounds, Terriers, Pinschers and Schnauzers, and Toy and Companion Breeds, and is intended to be used as an identification aid to many of the most common, and perhaps some of the more unusual breeds, and as an interesting guide to their origins and history, whilst also presenting information concerning the requirements and typical behavioural characteristics of many of the breeds discussed. Every detailed entry is accompanied by a number of concise points for quick reference, including the average height, weight, and key identifying features of each dog.

The origins of the domestic dog

The domestic dog is a carnivorous mammal that belongs to the family Canidae, which includes such animals as wild dogs and foxes, and more specifically, to the genus Canis, which includes the coyote, jackals and wolves. Furthermore, despite the vast diversity in its form, whereby several hundred distinct breeds are recognized today by various authorities, the domestic dog is usually designated as a single species, *Canis familiaris*; a descendant of the Grey Wolf, although some experts regard it as con-specific, or the same species as the Grey Wolf, but a domestic variant. Despite this, it is possible, perhaps even probable, that the progenitors of different breeds of domestic dog evolved independently out of the numerous subspecies of the Grey Wolf, which includes the Eastern Timber, Tundra, Arabian, Indian, Tibetan and Asian Desert Wolves, and it is also likely that domesticated dogs have interbred with their wild ancestors at various points in their development, contributing to the diversity between breeds. In fact, the dog has evolved a greater array of sizes, shapes and specializations than any other species, but it is undoubtedly man's intervention that has had the greatest effect in the shaping of the domestic dog. However, it should also be remembered that dogs have in no small way altered the history of man.

The history of domestication

Precisely when the association between man and dog, or man and wolf, first began is impossible to establish, but the dog was almost certainly the first animal to have been domesticated, and archaeological evidence, in the form of cave paintings, fossil records and excavations that reveal human and canine remains in close proximity, would seem to suggest that man has at least been interested in dogs for as long as 125,000–150,000 years, and probably far longer. Recent archaeological and genetic studies have yielded a wide range of results, placing the divergence of dogs from wolves at anywhere between 15,000 and 135,000 years ago, and sometimes point to a single gene pool and domestication event, but it is now largely accepted that the wolf-dog split probably occurred around 15,000–20,000 years ago during the Upper Paleolithic period, and that domestication took place independently across a huge geographic range.

Being a prehistoric event, a degree of speculation is required in order to attempt to reach an understanding of the domestication of the dog, but coupled with the scientific evidence, which points to the fact that man and wolves had been living side by side for many thousands of years, it is not difficult to imagine

how it may have taken place. Up until the Upper Paleolithic, and the beginning of the retreat of the huge ice sheets after the peak of the last ice age, both man and wolves had been largely nomadic hunters, following the seasonal migrations of large herds of herbivorous undulates, or hoofed mammals, and it is likely that wolves had long scavenged around the fringes of human encampments looking for an easy meal, whilst probably keeping other vermin and scavengers at bay, suggesting the beginnings of a relationship that was mutually beneficial. Therefore, by the end of the ice age, as man began to settle and abandon his nomadic ways, the value of the wolf as an ally had probably already been realized, and the first steps to adopting wolves into human society, and of wolves accepting man, had already been taken.

Both lived in relatively small social groups, typified by a companionate hierarchy, which ensured the success of such tasks as cooperative hunting and care of the young, and therefore the survival of the group, and the similarities between the natural social patterns, and other behaviours, of both man and wolves, coupled with a pre-existing acceptance between the species, no doubt engendered and ensured the success of domestication. For as man faced the new challenges of life after the last ice age, the canine instincts concerning loyalty, territory, hunting and even herding, would prove complementary to his own, and perhaps even invaluable to his survival.

Designing the dog

By the Neolithic period, man had succeeded in domesticating various wild cereal crops, such as rice, wheat and barley, as well as the progenitors of various animals that could now be regarded as livestock, from reindeer, to pigs, sheep and cattle, and as such, he had laid the foundations of a more settled agricultural existence. In spite of this, hunting continued to be an important means of acquiring food, and perhaps took on a new and significant function: that of protecting both crops and livestock from consumption by wild animals, whilst the development of the bow and arrow may have introduced new roles for dogs, namely, the flushing and locating of game. Crops and livestock may also have required protection from neighbouring or nomadic tribes, as would have homes and possessions, and as man adapted to these new ways of life, he was assisted, if not enabled, to do so by his domestication of, and alliance with, the dog. These new preoccupations of man brought new roles for the dog, which was by now firmly entrenched in human society, and archaeological evidence, which reveals conspicuous differences in the sizes and shapes of dogs, would seem to suggest that selective breeding had already begun as far back as 9,000–10,000 years ago, as dogs with particular characteristics were selected to perform specific tasks.

Simultaneously, as the relationship between man and dogs developed, and the value of dogs became increasingly apparent, man's affection for them undoubtedly grew and the bond strengthened, so that the companionship that a dog could offer was also recognized. However, as man became increasingly 'civilized', the heritage of the dog as a wild animal was not forgotten, and he remained aware that alongside the instincts that made the dog a useful asset, lay the potential for hostility and aggression, and feral dogs in particular, which had reverted to a semi-wild state, were usually feared. Meanwhile, in some cultures, including those that revered and valued them for many reasons, it was not uncommon for dogs to be eaten.

By Roman times, dogs were being employed in many of the same roles that they are to this day, including hunting, herding, guarding and as companions. Several recognizable types of dog had become established, whose early forms had most likely originated from different parent stocks in different locations, and which had been selectively bred to emphasize certain characteristics that made them best suited to particular tasks, often in particular conditions. For example, it is supposed that the long-jawed, lightly built, fast-running sighthounds, such as the Saluki, which had been employed to hunt by sight in the Middle Eastern deserts, may be descended from the Arabian Wolf, Canis lupus arabis, whilst the large, powerful mastiff-type dogs, known to the Romans as the Molossus, which were originally employed as guard dogs and dogs of war, are thought to have originally descended from the Tibetan Wolf, Canis lupus chanco, in the mountains of Tibet. The Romans were also the first to establish an extensive international trade in dogs, bringing the different types together, and disseminating them across their Empire and beyond, where new forms would gradually both evolve and be developed by selective breeding. However, the extreme morphological diversity seen in the domestic dog today, and by extension, the sheer number of different breeds that are recognized, is a relatively recent development in the history of both man and dog.

The modern dog

As civilizations and technologies spread and developed, and human needs, desires and activities changed, so new roles continued to be created for dogs, and many became increasingly specialized, from terriers designed to kill vermin or go to ground in the narrow passageways of animal burrows, to hounds required to track over long distances, mastiff and spitz-types used for draught work, and the gundogs, which were developed to hunt, point, flush and retrieve game for their human masters. Thus a process of continual refinement had been set in motion, whereby the physical attributes and temperamental or behavioural qualities of various types of dogs were combined, and types divided and sub-divided as man sought to perfect all kinds of dogs for all kinds of tasks.

By the 1800s, many of the dogs that we would recognize today were certainly in existence, but it was not until the late 19th century that they began to be classed as distinct breeds. This dramatic change was largely prompted by the formation of various canine appreciation societies or kennel clubs, which

began to keep stud books to record the bloodlines of various dogs, establish particular breed standards and provide an arena for exhibition and competitive display. Increasingly, as modernization and industrialization distanced man from nature, and some uses of dogs became more or less redundant, the popularity of dogs as pets or companions grew, whilst for some, they represented a means to partake in country pursuits, such as shooting or coursing, and for others, their true working ability, as hunters, herders or guardians, never really diminished.

Breed groupings

Although there are perhaps as many as 800 distinct breeds in existence, around 300 or so are officially, widely or commonly recognized by various kennel clubs as purebred, and most canine organizations, such as the British Kennel Club, American Kennel Club, United Kennel Club, and the World Canine

Organization, or Fédération Cynologique Internationale, largely continue to group breeds according to the roles that they were originally and specifically bred to fulfil. There are some differences between the designation of these groups and some which are further sub-divided; some authorities refer to the gundogs as the sporting dogs for example, make distinctions between types of hounds, or divide mastiffs, spitz-types and others, variously as working, utility or non-sporting dogs, sometimes resulting in a group of seemingly disparate breeds. Similarly, there are also some differences in the assignment of breeds to particular groups, often as the result of a variation in a dog's particular function, or perceived function, from country to country. Likewise, breed standards are also subject to some variation between one authority and another, be it regarding height and weight restrictions, coat types, colours and markings, or the somewhat more controversial subject of tail docking and the cropping of ears.

Physical characteristics, attributes and behaviour

Despite the huge diversity amongst domestic dog breeds, and the varied processes by which this diversity was attained, the domestic dog retains many of the physical, instinctual and behavioural attributes of its ancestor, the Grey Wolf. All dogs are essentially carnivorous predators and scavengers, with physical characteristics, senses, instincts and social bonds that are geared towards the hunting of other animals. It is these natural traits that have been enhanced and refined in various ways in order to produce the diversity seen in the domestic dog today.

Generally, dogs have keen senses of sight, smell and hearing, powerful muscles and a cardiovascular system that provides both speed and stamina. Their strong jaws and teeth are used for catching and holding prey, as well as for tearing flesh and gnawing bones. Dogs have a fairly flexible skeleton, are usually relatively long-limbed, and walk on their toes, affording them a greater degree of agility. They have also developed the capability of working cooperatively.

The senses: sight

Dogs have a wider field of vision than humans, on account of their eyes being positioned closer to the sides of their heads. In some sighthounds, which, as their name would suggest, rely most heavily on their vision when hunting, this field of vision may extend up to 270°. This compares to up to about 180° in some broader-headed breeds with more forward-facing eyes, and around 120° in humans. Dogs' eyes are also more sensitive to motion and light than the human eye, providing better vision when light levels are low, but dogs see in less detail than people, having flatter lenses. Although dogs were previously thought to be dichromatic (colour-blind), recent research has suggested that dogs may have limited colour vision.

Hearing

In general, dogs have very acute hearing, enabling them to locate each other and their quarry more easily. They are capable of hearing sounds as low as 16 Hz, and as high as 100,000 Hz, compared to a range of between about 20–20,000 Hz in humans. In many breeds, the ears are also highly mobile, enabling the rapid and precise location of a sound; dogs can also hear sounds over much longer distances than humans, around four times further. In recent years the hearing ability of dogs has been utilized in order to help the deaf; dogs are trained to alert their owners to particular sounds, such as a doorbell or telephone.

Scenting

Dogs have a highly advanced sense of smell, essential in tracking their intended quarry over long distances, and often through difficult terrain. It is mainly the scenthounds, such as the Bloodhound, that have been selectively bred for their excellent scenting abilities, and put to use in hunting and tracking. However, many of the gundog or sporting breeds also have a superb sense of smell, which is useful not only in locating game. Dogs such as Labrador Retrievers and various types of spaniel are employed by police, customs and military forces as sniffer dogs, used to detect narcotics and explosives. Dogs have millions more smell-sensitive cells than humans, but it is not only with their noses that they are able to locate and follow scents. They have an organ in the mouth known as Jacobson's Organ. It is thought that dogs can differentiate between two kinds of scent when tracking; an air scent, and a more permanent, but more easily contaminated ground scent.

Behaviour and communication

Perhaps amongst the most compelling reasons for the success of the relationship between man and dog lies in the fact that dogs, being reasonably intelligent and essentially social animals, have the ability to learn complex social behaviours. They can adapt and learn from new situations, and interpret and communicate with a variety of sounds and body language. In fact, dogs are far more adept at the delivery and perception of nonverbal cues by means of body language than humans, and are generally excellent at learning to read human body language. Dogs use a wide range of vocalizations and movements in order to communicate with other dogs, humans and other animals, including barking, growling, whining and howling; they may gesticulate by adopting particular positions with the entire body, or by moving specific parts, such as the head, mouth, ears, eyes, eyebrows and tail, often in various combinations. Dogs are also able to communicate by scent marking, either by spraying urine or by scratching at the ground to deposit sweat to mark territorial boundaries.

Most wild canines live in packs, which are bound together in a distinct hierarchy. Each member of the pack possesses a particular social rank, and displays of dominance and submission between pack members, which help to affirm and maintain social standing, are amongst the most common forms of dog communication. This behaviour is also carried over by dogs into their relationships with humans, and may be revealed in numerous ways. A submissive dog that feels particularly threatened will typically cower, with its head and ears held low, and its tail between its legs, or may roll onto its back. A dominant, aggressive dog will usually stand tall, with the head and neck extended, the tail erect, and the hairs along its back, which are known as its hackles, raised; the mouth may be held in a snarl, with the teeth exposed.

Tail movements
Although the natural position of a dog's tail varies from breed to breed, generally speaking, how high or low the tail is carried is often a good indication of a dog's mood and social position. A high tail typically indicates confidence and dominance, and a tail that is held low often suggests insecurity and submissiveness. Similarly, tail-wagging may reveal a dog's mood, with slow, small

wags thought to suggest that a dog is questioning or confused about a situation, and large, rapid tail movements indicating happiness, possibly tinged with a degree of submission.

Ear movements

Although less detectable in pendant-eared dogs than in prick-eared breeds, ear movements can also be an important means of communication between dogs. For example, erect, forward-facing ears would suggest that a dog is being highly attentive to a sound or situation. The position of the ears can also reveal a dog's mood. When the ears are held backwards against the head, for instance, this will often imply fear.

Facial expressions

The movements of a dog's mouth, eyes and eyebrows also provide an important means of communication. Certain expressions may appear quite similar to our own, and convey similar emotions. Raised eyebrows typically suggest curiosity; confusion or anger may be suggested by lowered brows, and suspicion by half-closed eyes. Yawning may simply indicate tiredness, but can also suggest a desire to be alone. An open mouth, with the lips relaxed, which may actually appear like a smile and be accompanied by panting, is generally a sign that a dog is happy and may wish to play. Snarling, with the lips pulled back to reveal the teeth, is commonly seen as a sign of aggression, but it may also be a playful gesture, and body language should be read as a whole in order to discern a dog's likely mood and possible intentions.

Vocalizations: barking

Interestingly, although the domestic dog is a subspecies of the Grey Wolf, it has a far larger repertoire of vocalizations than its ancestor. Barking in particular represents a major difference, for although wolves may bark in certain situations, barking tends to be more specific, isolated and brief. Dogs bark far more often, in response to a greater variety of stimuli, and in much longer, often rhythmic, patterns. It is thought that this tendency to bark may have been fostered during early domestication, representing a means by which humans could be alerted to the presence of intruders and potential predators. However, dogs bark for a wide variety of reasons: to attract attention, express surprise, for identification, and in play. They may reveal a wide range of emotions, including excitement, fear, stress and happiness, depending upon their tone.

Howling

As with its parent species, the Grey Wolf, the domestic dog uses howling as a means of long-distance communication. It may be employed to locate pack members and owners, and bring them together, but may also be used to announce their presence to other dogs, and deter them from intruding on their territory. Additionally, dogs may howl in response to particularly loud or high-pitched sounds, including music and alarms.

Growling

Although growling is often indicative of aggression and dominance, and may precede an attack by a dog, it is also used to express a desire to play. A playful dog that is growling may usually be distinguished from an aggressive dog on

account of it not snarling to expose its teeth; but caution should be exercised in such situations, and attention paid to other possible signals such as tail movements and overall body language.

Whining

Dogs may whine for several reasons; to attract attention, as an expression of pain or fear, and also when they are excited, such as when greeting people or other dogs.

Dogs as pets

Today, despite changes in farming and hunting methods, dogs still perform many of the tasks for which they were developed hundreds, if not thousands of years ago, but their versatility has seen them successfully employed in numerous new roles, from acting as guide dogs and hearing dogs for the blind and deaf, as assistance and therapy dogs for the disabled and ill, to crowd control, and the detection of narcotics, explosives and even mineral deposits. Recreationally, dogs continue to be shown competitively, and are able to exhibit some of their instinctive behaviours, whilst also demonstrating the deep relationship that has developed between dog and man, by participating in field, sheepdog, obedience and agility trials. However, it is perhaps as companions, or 'man's best friend', that dogs are most commonly encountered.

The relationship between man and dog as companions is typically characterized by a strong emotional bond, and often by an almost unconditional acceptance on the part of the dog, and it should therefore be recognized that most dogs, when kept as pets, not only require regular meals, exercise and grooming, which are among the more obvious practical considerations, but are generally also highly dependent upon human contact, and may suffer from anxiety and even poor health if deprived of such contact for extended periods. That said, to anthropomorphize that is, to attribute human intelligence and emotion to, or in any other way overindulge a dog, may also be problematic, and a responsible owner should ensure that a dog is both obedience trained and socialized with people and others of its kind when young, to avoid fearfulness or overdominance in later life, which might both otherwise lead to aggression.

HERDING
BREEDS

GIANT SCHNAUZER

The Giant Schnauzer, as its name might suggest, is the largest member of the three Schnauzer breeds and originated in southern Bavaria in Germany as a cattle herding dog, probably as the result of breeding between Standard Schnauzers, rough-coated cattle dogs, such as the Bouvier des Flandres, and possibly also black Great Danes. It was soon recognized for its guarding ability, and as with many herding breeds, was to prove itself as a highly versatile working dog. Today, in addition to being a loyal and affectionate companion, it is used by both the police and military in Germany and Holland, and also as a search and rescue dog. The Giant Schnauzer retains something of the temperament of a terrier, which can be problematic in a dog of this size. However, with consistent training and plenty of exercise, this energetic and intelligent breed makes an excellent pet.

HEIGHT: 58–71cm (23–28in)
WEIGHT: 25–36kg (55–80lb)
LIFE EXPECTANCY: 12–14 years
ORIGIN: Germany
DESCRIPTION: A large, powerful dog, with bushy eyebrows, whiskers and a beard. The tail is usually docked, and the ears sometimes cropped. The coat is composed of a soft, dense undercoat, and a harsh, wiry outer coat. It may be black or black and grey in colour

BOUVIER DES FLANDRES

Translated as the 'cowherd from Flanders', and often known simply as the Belgian Cattle Dog, the Bouvier des Flandres was developed as a working farm dog, used to herd and guard cattle, and also for draught work: pulling carts of farm produce. The exact origins of this breed are unknown, but it is thought to be related to the Beauceron and Dutch Griffon. Although there continues to be some dispute as to its heritage, it was developed in its present form in Belgium after the decimation of Flanders in the First World War. The Bouvier des Flandres was used extensively, in both major European conflicts, as a message and supply carrier and was almost wiped out as a breed, with the result that its present lineage can be traced to a small gene pool. Unfortunately, this initial close breeding continues to be associated with certain reproductive complications. However, in general, the breed is quite hardy, and makes a loyal pet, as well as being used for police work, search and rescue and as a guide dog.

HEIGHT: 56–71cm (22–28in)
WEIGHT: 27–41kg (59–90lb)
LIFE EXPECTANCY: 10–12 years
ORIGIN: Belgium
DESCRIPTION: A large, powerfully built dog, with a massive head and broad muzzle, emphasized by a prominent beard, moustache and eyebrows. The ears are triangular, the tail normally docked, and the coat is dense and wiry. Colours include black, grey, fawn and brindle

AUSTRALIAN CATTLE DOG

HEIGHT: 43–51cm (17–20in)
WEIGHT: 14–20kg (30–45lb)
LIFE EXPECTANCY: 12–15 years
ORIGIN: Australia
DESCRIPTION: A compact and muscular breed with a broad head, deep chest and a medium-length, slightly curving tail. The coat is short, dense and rough, and may be blue or red speckled or mottled, with black and tan markings

Originating from a mixture of several breeds, including collies, the Australian Kelpie, Dalmatian and native feral Dingoes, the Australian Cattle Dog was developed by 19th century settlers in order to herd cattle over long distances in inhospitable conditions. In doing so, they produced a highly intelligent, alert and bold dog with almost inexhaustible energy and stamina, which was willing and able to drive cattle quietly and efficiently. It does so by biting at the cattle's heels, which explains this breed's alternative names of Australian, Queensland or Blue, Heeler. Naturally protective of its charges, this instinct typically also extends to its owner and their property, making it an excellent guard dog, but being so athletic, it requires a great deal of space and exercise if it is to remain content as a non-working, family pet.

LANCASHIRE HEELER

Thought to have been developed from the Manchester Terrier and Welsh Corgis, possibly with the later addition of Dachshund stock, the Lancashire Heeler is a short-legged, slightly elongated, terrier-like dog, which was used as a vermin catcher, cattle herder and general farm dog, with the name Heeler being derived from the way that these dogs worked: nipping at the heels of the cattle in order to drive them forwards. However, a distinction is sometimes made between smaller and larger dogs, with the former being known as Butcher's Heelers, and the latter, which were more commonly found as herding dogs, and which sometimes also bore white markings, being known as Ormskirk Heelers. As the need for cattle dogs diminished with the growth of mechanized farming, the Lancashire Heeler was threatened with extinction, but it has since found favour as an affectionate and lively companion and watchdog.

HEIGHT: 25–31cm (10–12in)
WEIGHT: 4–6kg (8–14lb)
LIFE EXPECTANCY: 12–14 years
ORIGIN: Britain
DESCRIPTION: A low-set, short-legged dog, with a long body, large, wide-set ears and a high-set tail, which is carried over the back. The coat is black and tan, usually sleek and shiny, becoming somewhat longer in winter, with a noticeable mane

CARDIGAN WELSH CORGI

HEIGHT: 25–33cm (10–13in)
WEIGHT: 11–18kg (24–40lb)
LIFE EXPECTANCY: 12–14 years
ORIGIN: Britain
DESCRIPTION: An elongated, low-set dog, with a deep chest, very large, erect ears, and a long, low-set tail. The coat is of medium length, with a ruff around the neck, and colours include brindle, blue merle, black, black and tan, black and brindle, sable and red, often with white markings

The Welsh Corgi is certainly an old breed, having been recorded in the Domesday Book in 1086, but its origins are thought to be far older, and remain the subject of much speculation. Its name derives from the Celtic word for dog, and it may have descended from ancient Celtic breeds, whilst argument also continues as to whether it is the ancestor or descendant of the Swedish Vallhund. Of the two varieties of Welsh Corgi, the Cardigan Welsh Corgi is almost certainly the oldest. Both were employed as droving dogs, which worked by nipping at the heels of livestock, and until 1934, when they were officially recognized as distinct breeds, they were commonly interbred. With recognition came the application of distinct standards, and the accentuation of particular traits. Thus, the Cardigan Welsh Corgi may be distinguished by its heavier build, larger ears and brush-like tail.

PEMBROKE WELSH CORGI

Like the Cardigan Welsh Corgi, the Pembroke is an ancient, short-legged droving dog, which was employed to drive livestock such as sheep, cattle and ponies by biting at their heels. Today, however, both varieties are more commonly found as companions and watchdogs than as herding dogs, and both make affectionate pets, although the Pembroke is often regarded as more obedient, and has also been used as a retrieving gundog. The Pembroke Welsh Corgi is also the better known of the two breeds, and certainly the most popular, no doubt partly as the result of royal patronage, it being the favourite breed of Queen Elizabeth II. The Pembroke is most readily identified by its short or absent tail, and is generally smaller, with smaller ears and a more wedge-shaped head than the Cardigan Welsh Corgi.

HEIGHT: 25–30cm (10–12in)
WEIGHT: 10–12kg (22–26lb)
LIFE EXPECTANCY: 12–14 years
ORIGIN: Britain
DESCRIPTION: An elongated, low-set dog, with a fox-like head and large, erect ears. The tail is naturally short, but is sometimes completely docked. The coat is soft, and may be red, sable, fawn or black and tan, usually with white markings

GERMAN SHEPHERD DOG

Highly intelligent, responsive and versatile, the German Shepherd Dog, or Alsatian, is probably amongst the most familiar and popular of all dog breeds. It originated in Germany as a herding dog, but has since gone on to be employed worldwide by various police and military forces, used for search and rescue, as a guard dog, a guide dog for the blind, and as a family companion. It excels at obedience and agility trials, and also as a show dog. It was first shown in 1882, and for many years it was exhibited in its various forms, including white-coated and long-haired, but today only the short-haired German Shepherd is generally accepted at dog shows, and white is typically regarded as a disqualifying factor. However, whilst white German Shepherds became increasingly uncommon in Europe, they continued to proliferate in North America, and some authorities now recognize them as a distinct breed, designated as either the American White Shepherd, or simply as the White Shepherd.

HEIGHT: 55–65cm (22–26in)
WEIGHT: 34–43kg (75–95lb)
LIFE EXPECTANCY: 11–13 years
ORIGIN: Germany
DESCRIPTION: A large, muscular dog, with a slightly elongated body, long muzzle and long, bushy tail. The ears are large, triangular and erect. The coat is dense, may be short or long, and is typically black and tan in colour. White German Shepherds are sometimes regarded as a distinct breed

GROENENDAEL (BELGIAN SHEPHERD DOG)

HEIGHT: 56–66cm (22–26in)
WEIGHT: 27–34kg (59–75lb)
LIFE EXPECTANCY: 12–14 years
ORIGIN: Belgium
DESCRIPTION: A large, muscular, black sheepdog, with a long tapering muzzle and erect triangular ears. The coat is dense, of medium length, with a feathered underside, legs and tail, and a ruff around the neck

One of four closely related breeds that are also known simply as the Belgian Sheepdog or Belgian Shepherd Dog, the Groenendael is easily distinguished from the others by its black coat. However, some canine organizations do not recognize all four breeds, or consider them as being one and the same. An enthusiastic and energetic worker, in addition to herding, the Groenendael has been used as a guard dog, police dog and in search and rescue work, and it was employed in various roles during both World Wars, including the carrying of messages and supplies, and even towing machineguns on the battlefield. Of the four breeds, this dog is probably the most commonly found as a household pet and family companion, but it requires a great deal of exercise if not working, in which case, obedience or agility trials may provide a suitable alternative.

(BELGIAN SHEPHERD DOG) LAEKENOIS

Highly intelligent, watchful and obedient, before proving its worth as a sheepdog, this breed was used in Belgium's flax fields, guarding the crops and linen cloth that had been left outside to be bleached in the sun. It would later also become valued as a police and army dog, as well as being used for search and rescue work, and it makes a loyal family pet if well trained and socialized when young. However, it is an energetic dog, which requires plenty of exercise, and some individuals can become aggressive and uncooperative on account of their protective instincts. Although considered by many to be the foundation of the four Belgian sheepdog breeds, the Laekenois is the least common today, and whilst the Groenendael, Malinois and Tervuren are widely recognized as breeds in their own right, this is less true of the Laekenois.

HEIGHT: 56–66cm (22–26in)
WEIGHT: 27–34kg (59–75lb)
LIFE EXPECTANCY: 12–14 years
ORIGIN: Belgium
DESCRIPTION: A large, muscular sheepdog, with a long tapering muzzle and erect triangular ears. The coat is dense and wiry. Colours range from fawn to mahogany, often with black on the muzzle, ears and tail

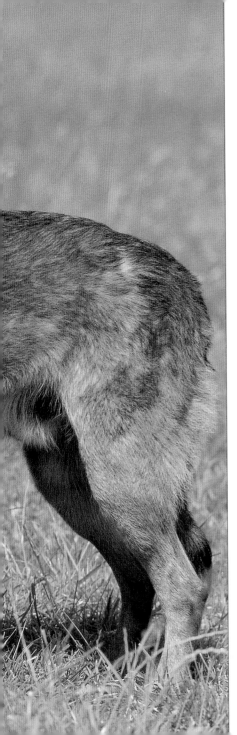

MALINOIS
(BELGIAN SHEPHERD DOG)

Developed as a herding dog around the city of Malines in Belgium, the Malinois is the only one of the four breeds, or varieties, of Belgian sheepdog that has a short coat. Both the Groenendael and Tervuren are long-haired, whilst the coat of the Laekenois is rough and wiry. The Malinois is much like the more familiar German Shepherd Dog in general appearance, although it is typically taller and more lightly built. Being similarly intelligent and versatile, today it excels in many of the same roles, including guarding, police and military work, search and rescue and as a therapy or guide dog. If firmly trained and well socialized when young, the Malinois will often also make an excellent family pet, but it can be wary with strangers and aggressive towards other animals at times. A very active and lively dog, it will also require plenty of exercise if it is to remain happy, and is not generally recommended for a first time dog owner.

HEIGHT: 56–66cm (22–26in)
WEIGHT: 27–34kg (59–75lb)
LIFE EXPECTANCY: 12–14 years
ORIGIN: Belgium
DESCRIPTION: A large, muscular sheepdog, with a long tapering muzzle and erect triangular ears. The coat is short, and fawn to reddish or grey in colour, with shading, a black-tipped tail, face and ears

TERVUREN (BELGIAN SHEPHERD DOG)

HEIGHT: 56–66cm (22–26in)
WEIGHT: 27–34kg (59–75lb)
LIFE EXPECTANCY: 12–14 years
ORIGIN: Belgium
DESCRIPTION: A large, muscular sheepdog, with a long tapering muzzle and erect triangular ears. The coat is medium to long, and composed of a dense, fawn undercoat with a black overlay. The rump and backs of legs are feathered, and a ruff is often present around the neck

Of the four Belgian sheepdogs, this breed, along with the Groenendael, is most commonly kept as a family pet, whilst the Laekenois and Malinois are more frequently used as guard dogs. However, it is still also employed as a herding dog, and excels in a variety of roles, from police work, search and rescue and sled pulling, to being used as a therapy and guide dog. Identical to the Groenendael except in colour, the Tervuren may be distinguished by its black-tipped outer coat and lighter undercoat, which produces a black overlay on the head, shoulders and back, providing an overall appearance that is somewhat reminiscent of a long-haired German Shepherd Dog. As with the other members of the Belgian shepherd dog group, this breed is naturally protective, intelligent and quick to learn, but requires a good deal of both mental and physical stimulation if it is to remain content.

AUSTRALIAN SHEPHERD DOG

Despite its name, the Australian Shepherd Dog originated in the US, and was developed from herding breeds of European origin. Many of these dogs were then exported to America and Australia during the 19th century. In both countries, these intelligent and incredibly hardworking dogs were initially employed on ranches and farms to herd sheep, but have since proven highly versatile, and whilst large numbers are still used to herd livestock, they also excel at retrieval, guarding, search and rescue and for police work. Instinctively protective, affectionate and loyal, the Australian Shepherd can make a rewarding family pet; however, it needs to be almost constantly active, and dogs from purely working lines may prove unsuitable in this role. Although not usually aggressive, this breed may also attempt to herd people by biting at their heels.

HEIGHT: 45–58cm (18–23in)
WEIGHT: 18–29kg (40–65lb)
LIFE EXPECTANCY: 12–15 years
ORIGIN: USA
DESCRIPTION: A medium-sized, but solid herding dog, with a medium-length coat, slightly feathered legs, and a naturally short tail. The ears are triangular, and set fairly high on the head. Coat and eye colour is highly variable

ROUGH COLLIE

Although today they are recognized as distinct breeds, both Rough and Smooth Collies were developed concurrently, and the difference in coat lengths is considered by many to be a natural variant. However, the Rough Collie has gone on to become the more popular of the two, no doubt on account of its luxuriant coat, and has undergone the most refinement. For whilst it is amongst the oldest of British herding breeds, today its working ability has undoubtedly been compromised by greater attention to its appearance, it having being bred for many years specifically, although not exclusively, as a show dog and companion. Some sources suggest that Greyhound, or perhaps Borzoi stock was introduced in order to provide a more refined, elongated head and muzzle. Intelligent, loyal and easy to train, the Rough Collie has also been employed as a rescue and guide dog, but is perhaps best known as the star of the 'Lassie' films.

HEIGHT: 51–61cm (20–26in)
WEIGHT: 23–34kg (50–75lb)
LIFE EXPECTANCY: 14–16 years
ORIGIN: Britain
DESCRIPTION: A fairly large, distinctive herding dog, with a long, tapering muzzle, erect ears that fold forwards at the tips, and a long, bushy tail. The coat is profuse, with a mane and frill about the neck and chest, and may be sable and white, black, white and tan or blue merle in colour

SHETLAND SHEEPDOG

First recognized in Britain in 1909, and registered with the British Kennel Club around five years later, the Shetland Sheepdog was formerly known as the Shetland, or Miniature Collie, and is very similar in appearance to the Rough Collie. It is thought to have been developed from that breed on the Scottish Shetland Islands, although a small Icelandic dog known as the Yakkin may also have contributed to its development there. Despite its somewhat dainty appearance, the Shetland Sheepdog is a hardy and hardworking dog, which was originally used to herd and guard livestock, often in inhospitable conditions, but today, on account of its attractive appearance, intelligence and gentle, obedient nature, it is highly popular as a show and companion breed. The Shetland Sheepdog also excels at competitive obedience, and can be taught to perform tricks.

HEIGHT: 30–38cm (12–15in)
WEIGHT: 5–8kg (12–18lb)
LIFE EXPECTANCY: 12–14 years
ORIGIN: Britain
DESCRIPTION: A fairly small, lightly built dog, with a long, wedge-shaped head, small erect ears that fold forward at the tips and a long, feathered tail. The coat is quite long, with a mane and frill around the neck, and may be blue merle, or sable and black with various amounts of white and tan

BORDER COLLIE

HEIGHT: 46–56cm (18–22in)
WEIGHT: 13–20kg (29–44lb)
LIFE EXPECTANCY: 12–15 years
ORIGIN: Britain
DESCRIPTION: A medium-sized, well proportioned sheepdog, with an alert expression and usually erect or semi-erect ears. The coat may be either short and sleek, or moderately long, and is most commonly black and white in colour

Highly intelligent, energetic and hardworking, the Border Collie was developed as a sheepdog in Northumberland, around the Scottish and English border, and is thought to be descended from a combination of old herding and spaniel stock. Incredibly responsive to training, today it is also employed in tracking, search and rescue and as a guide, assistance and sniffer dog, but it is still widely regarded as one of the best sheep-herding breeds ever developed, being eager to please, with unwavering stamina, agility and energy. The Border Collie also makes a fine companion but it requires a great deal of exercise and attention in order for it to remain happy, and if not employed as a working dog, then obedience, agility or sheepdog trials should be considered as an alternative outlet for this dog's boundless energy.

BEARDED COLLIE

Similar in appearance to the Old English Sheepdog, with a profuse covering of long hair and similar colouring, the Bearded Collie is thought to be descended from European sheepdogs such as the Polish Lowland Sheepdog, or Polish Owczarek Nizinny, as it is also known, that were first introduced to Scotland during the 16th century, and which were subsequently crossbred with local herding dogs. Used to this day to herd both cattle and sheep, this good natured, confident and affectionate breed is also a popular pet and successful show dog, but it prefers to be outdoors for much of the time, requires a great deal of exercise and also regular grooming to prevent matting of its coat. As the Border Collie gained favour in the early 20th century, the Bearded Collie drastically declined in numbers, almost to the point of extinction, but the breed was rescued during the 1940s.

HEIGHT: 50–56cm (20–22in)
WEIGHT: 18–27kg (40–60lb)
LIFE EXPECTANCY: 14–15 years
ORIGIN: Britain
DESCRIPTION: A medium-sized, herding dog with a shaggy coat. The coat typically changes colour throughout the dog's life, fading to grey from black, brown, fawn or blue, before darkening once more with maturity

OLD ENGLISH SHEEPDOG

HEIGHT: 51–61cm (20–24in)
WEIGHT: 27–41kg (60–90lb)
LIFE EXPECTANCY: 10–12 years
ORIGIN: Britain
DESCRIPTION: A large, muscular sheepdog, with a broad, deep chest and dense, shaggy coat. The ears are small and concealed by the coat, and the tail may be naturally absent or docked. The coat is usually blue, grey or blue merle, usually with white markings, or may be white with dark markings

A large, familiar breed, with a distinctive, shaggy coat, the Old English Sheepdog was developed in the English West Country during the 18th and 19th centuries, and it is thought that it is mainly descended from the Bearded Collie. However, several breeds have been suggested as possible ancestors, including the Briard, Bergamasco, Deerhound and a Russian breed, the Owtchar. As its name suggests, the Old English Sheepdog was employed mainly for herding sheep, but it was also used to drive cattle, and it has even been used to herd reindeer in colder climes, where it is well protected by its coat. At one time, this dog would have been shorn along with the sheep in the spring, but it is now more common as a companion and show breed than as a working dog, and requires regular grooming to maintain its appearance.

BRIARD

An ancient French Sheepdog, the Briard, or Berger de Brie, is thought to have originated in the 13th century, and was used both for herding and guarding livestock: work for which it is still employed to this day. However, being brave, intelligent and versatile, this breed has also been used by the French Army as a guard dog, and in wartime it has proven itself in various roles, from carrying messages, ammunition and other supplies, to the search and rescue of wounded soldiers. It suffered so many casualties that following the First World War, it was almost extinct, but fortunately, enough were spared to re-establish the breed. Today it is a popular family pet, as well as a working dog. Naturally protective and loyal, the Briard requires training and early socialization to prevent it from becoming too domineering and from trying to herd family members as well as other animals.

HEIGHT: 56–69cm (22–27in)
WEIGHT: 34–45kg (75–100lb)
LIFE EXPECTANCY: 10–12 years
ORIGIN: France
DESCRIPTION: A large, powerful sheepdog, with a long, coarse coat, shaggy eyebrows, beard and moustache. The tail is long and feathered, and the ears sometimes cropped. Two dewclaws are present on each hind foot. Coat colours include black, grey and tawny

BERGAMASCO

The Bergamasco is the only dog that has a coat composed of three layers: a short, oily undercoat, long 'goat hair', and a woolly outer coat, and it is the latter two that mat together to form cords or flocks, providing this large sheepdog with a unique and striking appearance. This dense coat serves to protect the Bergamasco from the elements, and at one time would have also afforded a degree of protection from wolves and other predators whilst it was guarding flocks of sheep. As a puppy, the coat is soft and fluffy, but it begins to develop into cords after about a year, and may reach the ground by the time the dog is about five years old. This dog originated in the Bergamo region, close to Milan, and was largely confined to Italy for many years. More recently it has gained in popularity in both Europe and the US, where it is now found as a guard dog, therapy dog and family companion.

HEIGHT: 55–60cm (22–24in)
WEIGHT: 26–32kg (57–84lb)
LIFE EXPECTANCY: 12–14 years
ORIGIN: Italy
DESCRIPTION: A medium-sized but powerfully built dog, with a distinctive matted, corded or flocked coat, which is mainly wiry at the front, more woolly towards the back, and may be grey, black or fawn in colour

PULI

HEIGHT: 38–46cm (15–18in)
WEIGHT: 9–16kg (20–35lb)
LIFE EXPECTANCY: 12–14 years
ORIGIN: Hungary
DESCRIPTION: A medium-sized, but fairly muscular dog with a distinctive corded coat. The ears are medium-sized and pendant, and the tail typically carried curled over the back. Coat colours include black, grey, apricot and white

The Puli is an ancient Hungarian sheepdog, which, like the closely related Komondor, is thought to have descended from an ancient Tibetan ancestor that was introduced to Hungary by the nomadic Magyars. Like the Komondor, the Puli possesses a highly distinctive, corded coat, which may reach to the ground by the time the dog is fully grown, and whilst it requires little grooming, it is generally advised to separate the matted hair into neat cords as they develop. The Puli was originally used as a sheep herder, rather than guardian, and darker coat colours were favoured in order to easily distinguish the dog from the flock, but today several colours occur, including white. The Puli had almost died out by the end of World War II, but was restored by a world-wide breeding programme, and has become increasingly popular as a family pet.

BEAUCERON

A possible ancestor of the Dobermann, this powerful black and tan dog was first used in France to hunt wild boar, before being employed to herd and guard livestock. Calm and highly obedient once trained, more recently this dog saw action in both World Wars, where it performed a variety of tasks, from carrying messages to mine detection, and today it is widely regarded as being one of the most versatile of all working dogs. Amongst other roles, it continues to be used as a sheepdog and guard dog, and by the French military and police forces, as well as for search and rescue. Originally not widely known outside France, it has gained in popularity in other parts of Europe and in the US as a watchdog and family companion. Slow to mature, the Beauceron requires socialization and firm handling from an early age, but in time will become a loyal and very protective pet.

HEIGHT: 60–70cm (24–28in)

WEIGHT: 29–50kg (65–110lb)

LIFE EXPECTANCY: 10–12 years

ORIGIN: France

DESCRIPTION: A large muscular dog, with distinctive double dewclaws on the hind legs. The coat is short overall, with fringing on the flanks and tail, and is either black and tan, or black, tan and grey. The ears are often cropped and erect

WORKING
BREEDS

MASTIFF

HEIGHT: 69–76cm
(27–30in)
WEIGHT: 72–86kg
(160–190lb)
LIFE EXPECTANCY: 10–12
years
ORIGIN: Britain
DESCRIPTION: A massive
dog, with a square
head and short muzzle.
The pendant ears lie
close to the cheeks, the
tail is high-set and
tapering. The coat is
short, and may be
golden, fawn, or
brindle, with a black
mask and dark ears

Although Mastiff-type dogs were known to the ancient
civilizations of the Middle East and the Orient, and
were employed by the military forces of the ancient
Greeks and Romans, the Mastiff was already established
in Britain by the time the Roman legions arrived in 43
AD, and it is thought that it may have been introduced
by Phoenician traders as early as the 6th century BC.
One of the heaviest and most powerful of dogs, the
Mastiff has been used at various times in its long history
as a war dog, fighting dog, bull- and bear-baiter, big
game hunter, livestock, property and personal guardian
and companion, but despite its imposing size, and
undoubted ability as a guard dog, it tends to have a
calm and steady temperament. However, it should be
thoroughly socialized when young, as it can otherwise
be aggressive towards other dogs.

BULLMASTIFF

As its name might suggest, the Bullmastiff is the result of crossbreeding between Mastiffs and Bulldogs, and it was originally developed in England during the 1800s as a gamekeepers' dog, used to protect country estates and their game from poachers. Despite its formidable appearance, it was trained not to maul or bite, but to find, overpower and restrain intruders, and this behaviour would go on to make it a popular watchdog, guard dog and police dog, long after the need for gamekeepers' dogs waned. Although it is less commonly employed as a working guard dog today, it is however found as a loyal family guardian and companion. Typically docile unless confronted, the Bullmastiff is nevertheless an alert and protective breed, and although it will not usually attack without provocation, it is highly powerful and can be wilful, and should be thoroughly trained and socialized when young.

HEIGHT: 61–69cm (24–27in)
WEIGHT: 41–59kg (90–130lb)
LIFE EXPECTANCY: 8–10 years
ORIGIN: Britain
DESCRIPTION: A very powerfully built Mastiff, with a broad head and short, square muzzle. The triangular ears are pendant and wide-set. The tail is high-set, but long and tapering. The coat is short, slightly rough, and may be brindle, fawn or red, often with black ears and muzzle

NEAPOLITAN MASTIFF

Most, if not all, European Mastiffs are thought to share an ancient Tibetan ancestor, which was taken from Asia to Greece by Alexander the Great around 300 BC, before being introduced to the Romans. However, it has also been suggested that Mastiffs were first introduced to Europe by the Phoenicians. Either way, the Neapolitan Mastiff is known to have descended from the Molossus, a Mastiff-type dog that was well known in ancient Rome, where it was used as a war and gladiatorial dog, and whilst the Neapolitan Mastiff has also seen action as a fighting breed, other uses include police work, draught work, guarding and companionship. Despite its formidable size and strength, the Neapolitan Mastiff of today is usually peaceful and affectionate, although it can be wary of strangers and will protect its owner fearlessly if necessary.

HEIGHT: 60–75cm (24–30in)
WEIGHT: 50–74kg (110–165lb)
LIFE EXPECTANCY: 8–10 years
ORIGIN: Italy
DESCRIPTION: A huge, heavily built dog with a massive head, wrinkled face and neck, and prominent dewlap. The ears are traditionally cropped short, and the thick tail is docked by a third. The coat is short and dense, and may be blue, black, cream or chocolate in colour, and may be solid or brindle

FILA BRASILEIRO

HEIGHT: 64–76cm (25–30in)
WEIGHT: 45–68kg (100 –150lb)
LIFE EXPECTANCY: 9–11 years
ORIGIN: Brazil
DESCRIPTION: A powerful Mastiff-type, with a long muzzle and pendulous skin, particularly on the head and neck. The ears and tail are long. The coat is short and smooth, and may be fawn, black or brindle, often with a black mask, and white markings on the feet, chest and tail-tip

Also known as the Brazilian Mastiff, the Fila Brasileiro is a huge, powerful dog, which is descended from old English Mastiff, Bloodhound, Bulldog and Portuguese herding stock. It originated in Brazil, where it was used for herding cattle, guarding livestock and property, and hunting big game. It tends to hold its quarry or an intruder at bay rather than immediately attacking, but it is exceptionally brave, will not back down from a confrontation, and if provoked, will instinctively target the head or neck of an aggressor. It is famed for its aggression to strangers, which is known as 'ojeriza', and although some breeders have attempted to produce a more amenable Fila Brasileiro, this trait is deeply ingrained, and begins to be exhibited when the dog is only a few months old. Despite this, it is invariably incredibly loyal and affectionate to its owner and family.

GREAT DANE

Despite its name, the Great Dane is of German, rather than Danish, origin and it is believed to have been developed from ancient Mastiffs introduced by the Romans which were subsequently crossbred with the Greyhound. A hugely powerful and athletic dog, it was first employed to hunt for large game such as deer, bear and wild boar, which earned it the alternative name of the German Boarhound. It became popular during the 1800s, as both a hunting dog and estate guardian, at which time it was further refined by a process of selective breeding. Although it is highly imposing, it tends to have a steady temperament, becoming aggressive only when necessary. An affectionate companion, the Great Dane requires socialization and obedience training when young, as a dog of this size may otherwise be unmanageable when fully grown.

HEIGHT: 71–86cm (28–34in)
WEIGHT: 45–68kg (100–150lb)
LIFE EXPECTANCY: 8–10 years
ORIGIN: Germany
DESCRIPTION: A very large, elegant dog, with a long, muscular neck, and long, blunted muzzle. The tail is long and tapering, and the high-set ears usually folded forwards, although they may be cropped and erect. The coat is short and sleek, and may be fawn, black, blue, brindle, harlequin or merle

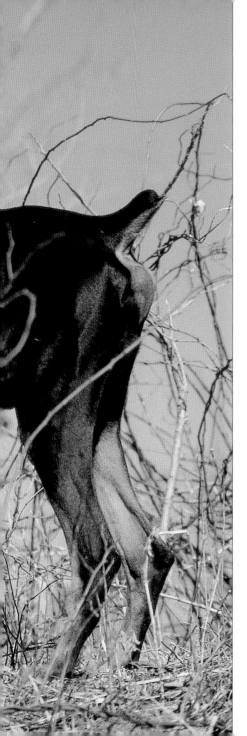

DOBERMANN PINSCHER

Usually known in Britain simply as the Dobermann, and elsewhere as the Dobermann Pinscher, this breed was developed in Germany during the 1860s by a tax collector, Louis Dobermann, who was seeking to create the perfect guard dog, and it is thought that the German Pinscher, Manchester Terrier, Rottweiler and Beauceron were probably amongst the most significant contributors to its development. The Dobermann is highly intelligent and assertive, and whilst it does indeed excel as a guard dog, it is usually not overly aggressive, and makes for a very loyal, protective and affectionate pet if it is well socialized when young. This incredibly versatile breed is also very responsive to training, and has been successfully employed as a police and military dog, herding farm dog, hunter, tracker and retriever, in search and rescue, and perhaps somewhat surprisingly given its origins, as a guide and therapy dog.

HEIGHT: 61–71cm (24–28in)
WEIGHT: 30–40kg (66–88lb)
LIFE EXPECTANCY: 10–12 years
ORIGIN: Germany
DESCRIPTION: A lean and elegant, but also square-bodied and muscular dog. Its coat is short and hard, and may be black or blue-grey with tan markings. The ears are some-times cropped and the tail usually docked very short

ROTTWEILER

HEIGHT: 56–68cm (22–27in)
WEIGHT: 36–59kg (80–130lb)
LIFE EXPECTANCY: 10–12 years
ORIGIN: Germany
DESCRIPTION: A large, muscular Mastiff-type dog, with a broad head and powerful muzzle. The ears are relatively small and fold forwards, and the tail is customarily docked short. The coat is short and dense, and black with tan markings on the face and feet

A very muscular, powerful breed, the Rottweiler originates from Rottweil in southern Germany, where it was developed from local shepherds' dogs and Mastiffs, and where it was used for guarding and cattle droving. It underwent a serious decline during the 19th century, but was revived by enthusiasts and organizations that recognized its potential in various roles, notably for police and military work. Today it is common throughout much of Europe, and is also one of the most popular breeds in the US. The Rottweiler was first introduced to Britain during the 1930s, where it has become favoured as a guard dog and companion, but elsewhere, notably in Scandinavia, this breed is also used for draught work and employed in mountain rescue. Although usually placid, the Rottweiler can be territorial and domineering and is generally not recommended for inexperienced owners.

DOGUE DE BORDEAUX

Also known as the French Mastiff, this powerfully built dog originated in France, and is amongst the oldest of French breeds. It is descended from ancient Mastiffs and has been used for hunting large game such as boar, as a war dog, for dog fighting, bull- and bear-baiting, herding and guarding. At one time there were three distinct types, the Paris, Toulouse and Bordeaux, and it is from the latter that today's Dogue de Bordeaux is descended, the breed having become almost extinct by the end of the Second World War. Once far more aggressive, selective breeding has resulted in a more even temperament, and the Dogue de Bordeaux is typically highly loyal and gentle with those that it knows, although it can be confrontational with other dogs and strangers. Whilst this breed is generally hardy, a caesarean section is often necessary when birthing, on account of the massive heads of the pups.

HEIGHT: 58–71cm (23–28in)
WEIGHT: 45–68kg (100–150lb)
LIFE EXPECTANCY: 10–12 years
ORIGIN: France
DESCRIPTION: A relatively short, stocky Mastiff, with a very large head. The lower jaw is undershot, the ears pendant, and the tail is long and tapering. The coat is short and occurs in shades of brown, with a black or red mask, and often some white on the feet and chest

(ENGLISH)
BULLDOG

The national dog of Great Britain, the Bulldog was originally developed from powerful Mastiff-type dogs, as a bull-baiting breed (hence its name) but following the prohibition of bull-baiting in 1835, when dog fighting would become increasingly popular, terrier blood was introduced to produce the more agile Bull Terrier, and the Bulldog began to lose favour with many owners. However, aware of its decline, certain individuals began to make efforts to ensure the survival of the breed, and many years of selective breeding would result in the less aggressive, but still formidable-looking Bulldog that we know today. Highly affectionate, the Bulldog is considered by many to be amongst the gentlest of dogs, and it makes a rewarding family companion. However, it can be susceptible to a range of ailments, including breathing difficulties, and pups are often required to be delivered by caesarean section due to their massive heads.

HEIGHT: 30–41cm (12–16in)
WEIGHT: 22–25kg (49–55lb)
LIFE EXPECTANCY: 8–10 years
ORIGIN: Britain
DESCRIPTION: A small and compact, but highly muscular dog, with a very large head, short, Pug-like muzzle and loose-fitting skin. The ears are usually folded back and the tail is short. The coat is short and may be red, fawn, white, brindle or any combination of those colours

AMERICAN BULLDOG

HEIGHT: 50–71cm (20–28in)
WEIGHT: 27–54kg (60–120lb)
LIFE EXPECTANCY: 12–15 years
ORIGIN: USA
DESCRIPTION: Compact and muscular, with powerful shoulders, neck, head and jaws, and a tapering tail. The coat is short, and colours include brindle, brown, red or tan, usually with large areas of white

The exact origin of the American Bulldog remains a contentious issue, but its ancestry is thought to lie, at least in part, in a form of working Bulldog, descended from ancient Mastiffs, that was taken from Britain to North America by early colonists, and which would later be bred with Bulldogs that were exported there after bull-baiting was outlawed in England in 1835. By the 1940s, the breed had almost died out, but it was carefully resurrected, primarily through the efforts of two principal breeders, John D. Johnson and Alan Scott. Still valued as a working dog, the American Bulldog continues to be a useful hunter, guard and farm dog, which exhibits intelligence, determination and protectiveness. As a pet it is generally lively and affectionate, but it may instinctively exhibit aggression towards other animals and strangers, and requires a great deal of exercise if it is to remain content.

BOXER

The Boxer was developed in Germany from two Mastiff-type dogs which were originally used for hunting large game and in the sports of bull- and bear baiting. These were crossed with the English Bulldog to produce the Boxer, which was also used in baiting and as a guard dog, but successive breeding has resulted in a more agile, less aggressive and more obedient breed, that has been used by the police and military, in search and rescue and also as a guide dog for the blind. Today it is common as a loyal and affectionate family pet, and although not usually aggressive, it retains an exuberant, boisterous and inquisitive personality, and should be well socialized from a young age in order to prevent it from becoming too dominant or stubborn. Its name is derived from its tendency to use its front paws when fighting or playing.

HEIGHT: 53–63cm (21–25in)
WEIGHT: 23–32kg (50–70lb)
LIFE EXPECTANCY: 12–14 years
ORIGIN: Germany
DESCRIPTION: A lean, but muscular Mastiff-like dog, with a broad chest, slightly upturned lower jaw, and wrinkled muzzle. The coat is short and sleek, and usually red, fawn or brindle in colour, often with a black mask and areas of white. The tail is usually docked

TOSA INU

Also known as the Tosa Ken, or in the West, as the Japanese Fighting Dog, this powerful Mastiff-type dog was, as its name might suggest, originally bred for the practice of dog fighting. It was developed by crossbreeding between native Kochi and Shikoku dogs, which were later bred with European dogs such as the Great Dane, Bulldog, Bull Terrier and various Mastiffs, to produce a massive, agile and relentless breed, although in Japan, the Tosa Inu tends to be smaller than those dogs found in the West. A rare breed, which has only recently been introduced to many countries, the Tosa Inu has already been banned in some, including Britain, as it is regarded as a dangerous dog. However, with proper training and control it can be both a good guard dog and family companion, although it tends to be aggressive towards other dogs, and requires a strong and experienced owner.

HEIGHT: 61–66cm (24–26in)
WEIGHT: 38–90kg (85–200lb)
LIFE EXPECTANCY: 10–12 years
ORIGIN: Japan
DESCRIPTION: A large, Mastiff-type dog, with a broad skull, square muzzle and loose skin around the neck. The ears are quite small and pendant, and the tail is tapering, being very thick at the base. The coat is short and harsh, and usually red, but may be black, black and tan, fawn, brindle or multi-coloured

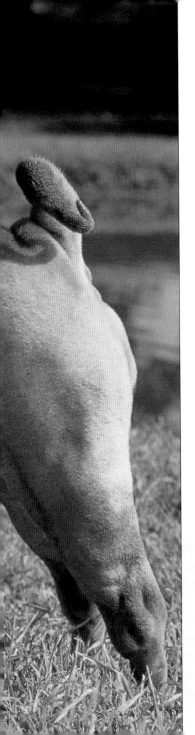

(CHINESE)
SHAR PEI

Although the exact origins of the Shar Pei are unclear, it is thought that it may be the result of crossbreeding between ancient Mastiffs and Nordic hunting dogs, and a link has been suggested with the Chow Chow on account of its blue-black tongue. There is certainly a resemblance between the 'bear-coated' form of the Shar Pei and the Chow Chow, although the latter is thought to be a far more ancient breed. The most distinctive features of the Shar Pei are its heavily wrinkled skin and rough coat (in fact its name literally translates as 'sand skin'), which were probably developed to aid in dog fighting, for which this breed was once extensively used. However, it has also served as a hunter, farm and guard dog. By the 1970s, the Shar Pei was almost extinct, being officially recognized as the rarest dog in the world during that decade, but an appeal by a breeder in Hong Kong prompted interest in the West, assuring its survival as a loyal, though somewhat independent companion.

HEIGHT: 46–51cm (18–20in)
WEIGHT: 18–27kg (40–60lb)
LIFE EXPECTANCY: 8–10 years
ORIGIN: China
DESCRIPTION: A fairly large, powerfully built dog, with a wide muzzle and heavily wrinkled skin. The ears are small and folded forwards, the tail high-set and curled. There are three coat varieties: a rough 'horse-coat', smoother 'brush-coat' and long 'bear-coat'. The 'bear-coat' is regarded as a fault in some competitive shows. Colours range from sandy to black

KOMONDOR

HEIGHT: 65–81cm (26–32in)
WEIGHT: 36–59kg (80–125lb)
LIFE EXPECTANCY: 10–12 years
ORIGIN: Hungary
DESCRIPTION: A very large dog with a distinctive, corded, white coat. The head and muzzle are heavy and somewhat short. The ears are pendant and the tail quite long, but both are concealed beneath the coat

Like the closely related, but much smaller Puli, the Komondor possesses a highly distinctive, corded coat. The two breeds may have descended from an ancient Tibetan ancestor that was introduced to Hungary by the nomadic Magyars. However, it has also been suggested that the Komondor is a direct descendant of the Aftscharka. Employed as a flock guardian, the Komondor's coat would have offered protection against both the elements and potential predators. The cords begin to form at around nine months, taking perhaps two years to fully develop, and they may reach the ground by the time the dog is around five years of age. Naturally protective, the Komondor should be well socialized when young, in order to prevent possible aggression to strangers in later life.

ANATOLIAN SHEPHERD DOG

Also known as the Karabash, meaning 'black head', and as the Turkish Guard Dog, the Anatolian Shepherd Dog is an ancient breed, native to Asia Minor, where it has been used as a livestock guardian for thousands of years, defending sheep from predators such as bears and wolves. It is instinctively protective, making it a loyal family pet and a good guard dog, but it is also strongly independent, may be wary of strangers and aggressive towards other dogs. Therefore, socialization and obedience training is recommended from a young age. Powerfully built, the Anatolian Shepherd Dog is also fast and agile and, whilst it continues to be employed as a sheepdog, it is also used for hunting, search and rescue, and by the military.

HEIGHT: 70–80cm (28–32in)
WEIGHT: 36–68kg (80–150lb)
LIFE EXPECTANCY: 12–15 years
ORIGIN: Turkey
DESCRIPTION: A large, muscular breed, with a broad head and rectangular muzzle. The ears are relatively small, triangular and pendant, but in Turkey are often cropped. The tail is carried over the back when alert. The coat is of medium length, and usually fawn in colour, with a dark mask, although variations include white and brindle

KUVASZ

A probable relative of the Komondor, the Kuvasz was also developed in Hungary, and may share a common ancestor, which is thought to have been taken into Europe from Tibet, via Turkey, and which is likely to have contributed to the development of other large flock guardians, such as the Great Pyrenees, Maremma Sheepdog, Akbash Dog and the Anatolian Shepherd Dog. As well as guarding livestock, this powerful breed has also been used for hunting large game, such as bears and wild boar, but today it is most commonly found as a companion and family guard dog. The Kuvasz is intelligent, and naturally protective, but it is also highly independent, and should be thoroughly socialized and trained when young, as adults may otherwise become territorial and domineering, with a tendency towards aggression, particularly to other dogs. This breed also requires vigorous regular exercise in order to prevent it from becoming restless and destructive.

HEIGHT: 65–81cm (26–32in)
WEIGHT: 36–59kg (80–125lb)
LIFE EXPECTANCY: 10–12 years
ORIGIN: Hungary
DESCRIPTION: A muscular, white dog with a tapering, but not pointed muzzle. The ears are folded and held close to the head, and the tail is long and carried low. The coat is of medium length, usually quite wavy, with a thick undercoat, forming a mane around the neck and chest

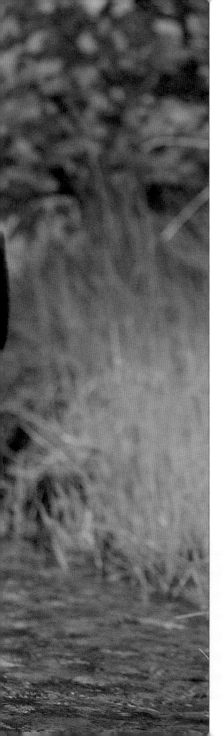

GREAT SWISS MOUNTAIN DOG

As its name would suggest, the Great Swiss Mountain Dog is a large breed which originated in the mountain villages and farms of the Swiss Alps, where it was used for draught work and cattle droving for hundreds of years. Whilst it is similar in appearance to the other Swiss mountain dogs, or sennenhunds, which include the Appenzell, Entlebuch and Bernese Mountain Dogs, it may be distinguished by its larger size. Like those breeds, it is thought to be descended from ancient Mastiffs, which were probably introduced to the area by the Romans, and it may also have played a part in the development of the St Bernard. Somewhat ironically, it was the popularity of that breed that led to a decline in its numbers. However, smooth-haired St Bernard stock was then used in order to help re-establish the Great Swiss Mountain Dog. Despite its imposing appearance, and its ability as a watchdog, the Great Swiss Mountain Dog is not aggressive, and enjoys human companionship.

HEIGHT: 61–72cm (24–29in)
WEIGHT: 59–61kg (130–135lb)
LIFE EXPECTANCY: 10–12 years
ORIGIN: Switzerland
DESCRIPTION: A large, muscular dog with a broad head, deep chest and slightly elongated body. The ears are medium-sized, pendant and triangular. The tail is long. The double-layered coat is dense, black overall, with tan on the face and legs, and white markings on the muzzle, chest, feet and tail-tip

GREAT PYRENEES

HEIGHT: 63–81cm (25–32in)
WEIGHT: 38–57kg (85–25lb)
LIFE EXPECTANCY: 11–13 years
ORIGIN: France
DESCRIPTION: A very large, muscular dog. The head is wedge-shaped, with a wide muzzle, the ears triangular and pendant, and the feathered tail curves upwards at the tip. The coat is dense, long and coarse, and may be white, or white with tan, grey or yellowish patches

Also known as the Pyrenean Mountain Dog, the Great Pyrenees is a huge, powerful breed that was developed in the Pyrenees Mountains from ancient Mastiffs, and it is thought to share a common ancestry with the Pyrenean Mastiff, Kuvasz and Anatolian Shepherd Dog. It was employed as a livestock guardian, defending flocks of sheep from potential predators such as bears and wolves, and although it is still found in that role today, it has also been used in mountain rescue, draught work, and as a family companion and guard dog. The Great Pyrenees is typically affectionate with those that it knows, but whilst its temperament is thought to be gentler than it once was, it is still highly imposing on account of its size, may be somewhat wary of strangers and aggressive with other dogs. Early socialization and training is recommended if this dog is to be kept as a pet.

BERNESE MOUNTAIN DOG

Also known as the Berner Sennenhund, the Bernese Mountain Dog is one of four Swiss mountain dogs, all of which share a similar general appearance. This breed may be distinguished from the others by its longer coat. Descended from sheepdog and Mastiff stock, the Bernese Mountain Dog was originally used to herd cattle and other livestock, and as a guard dog, but it is probably best known as a draught animal, used by weavers and farmers to pull carts of produce. Today it is occasionally encountered in a similar role, giving rides to young children, but it continues to be found as herder and guard dog, is employed in search and rescue work, and makes an affectionate and attentive companion. Unfortunately, the Bernese is highly susceptible to various forms of cancer, and in recent years, the life expectancy of this breed has decreased dramatically.

HEIGHT: 58–71cm (23–28in)
WEIGHT: 36–50kg (80–110lb)
LIFE EXPECTANCY: 6–8 years
ORIGIN: Switzerland
DESCRIPTION: A large, powerfully built and heavy dog, with broad head and deep chest. The ears are triangular and pendant, and the tail long and bushy. The coat is silky, of medium length, black in colour with a white muzzle, chest, feet and tail-tip, with chestnut or tan markings on the face and legs

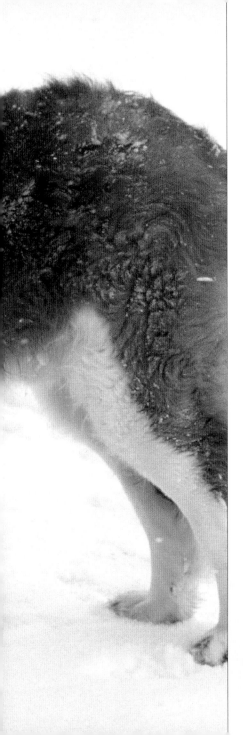

SAINT BERNARD

Formerly known as the Alpine Mastiff, the Saint Bernard is an old breed that is descended from the ancient Molossus, which was introduced to the Alps by the Romans around 2000 years ago. It was subsequently developed by monks at a travellers' refuge, the Hospice of St Bernard, from which its name is derived. First used as a guard dog and mountain guide, it began to be employed as a mountain rescue dog as long ago as the 17th century, and is perhaps best known for that role. However, with the construction of the Simplon Tunnel in 1905, which connects Switzerland and Italy, the mountains became more easily passable, and the Saint Bernard became more popular as a companion, although it is still used for rescue and draught work. Despite its imposing size, this is an extremely passive and affectionate breed, which is usually easy to train.

HEIGHT: 65–90cm (26–36in)
WEIGHT: 54–91kg (120–200lb)
LIFE EXPECTANCY: 10–12 years
ORIGIN: Switzerland
DESCRIPTION: A very large, muscular dog, with a powerful head and jaws. The ears are quite large and pendant, and the tail long and high-set. There are two types of coat, rough and smooth, but both are dense and white with tan, red, mahogany and black markings, in various combinations

NEWFOUNDLAND

Although it is named after the Canadian island of Newfoundland, there is some speculation that this breed did not actually originate there, but may have developed from large European Mastiffs, which were taken to Canada by the Vikings or by later settlers and fishermen. Others believe the Newfoundland to be closely related to the Labrador Retriever, and although the Newfoundland is a much larger dog, the two breeds share similar traits, including partially webbed feet and a love of water. Both were initially employed by fishermen to help haul in nets and retrieve lost tackle. The Newfoundland is also credited with saving the lives of fishermen that had fallen overboard, and was used to pull carts of fish to markets. Today it is most commonly encountered as a companion. In the US and Britain, the black and white form is regarded merely as a colour variety, but in much of Europe, it is designated as a distinct breed, known as the Landseer.

HEIGHT: 63–74cm (25–29in)
WEIGHT: 45–68kg (100–150lb)
LIFE EXPECTANCY: 8–10 years
ORIGIN: Canada
DESCRIPTION: A massive dog with a broad, heavy head and fairly short, square muzzle. The ears are triangular and pendant, and the tail is long and bushy. The coat is dense, of medium length, and may be black, black and blue, bronze, brown, grey or black and white in colour

TIBETAN MASTIFF

HEIGHT: 61–71cm (24–28in)
WEIGHT: 64–78kg (140–170lb)
LIFE EXPECTANCY: 14–16 years
ORIGIN: Tibet
DESCRIPTION: A powerful Mastiff-type dog, with a massive head. The ears are pendant, and the plumed tail is usually carried curled over the back. The medium-length coat is dense, with a ruff around the neck, and is typically dark, with gold or tan markings

An ancient breed, the Tibetan Mastiff may have been in existence in its earliest form since the stone or bronze age, and having been disseminated throughout Europe by the forces of Alexander the Great, it is thought to be the ancestor of most, if not all European Mastiffs. In Tibet itself, however, the breed stayed in relative isolation for hundreds of years, and so remained largely unchanged, and unknown to the outside world, until being popularized in Britain during the 19th century, where it was refined and standardized. Originally employed as a livestock guardian, the Tibetan Mastiff makes an excellent guard dog on account of its imposing size, fearlessness and protective nature, but it is generally docile, affectionate and even-tempered, its more aggressive tendencies having been reduced through successive breeding.

ALASKAN MALAMUTE

Amongst the oldest of the Nordic or Arctic sled dogs, the Alaskan Malamute is a descendant of the Arctic Wolf, and takes its name from a native Innuit tribe, known variously as the Malamute, Mahlemut or Malmuit indians, who domesticated it several thousand years ago. This dog was used to pull sleds which contained their food and various other supplies, and in more recent times, the Alaskan Malamute has been essential to the success of many polar expeditions. It is well adapted to such tasks, displaying great strength and stamina, and it is protected from the extreme cold by its dense, double-layered coat. Friendly and companionable, this breed also makes a good pet, but it is strong and active, and can be aggressive towards unfamiliar dogs or other small animals, and therefore requires firm handling and plenty of exercise.

HEIGHT: 56–71cm (22–28in)
WEIGHT: 36–54kg (80–120lb)
LIFE EXPECTANCY: 12–15 years
ORIGIN: USA
DESCRIPTION: A large, powerfully built Arctic dog, with a broad chest, head and muzzle, erect ears, and a well-furred tail, typically carried over its back. The coat is dense, and varies in colour from light grey to black, sometimes with shades of red. The underparts are white

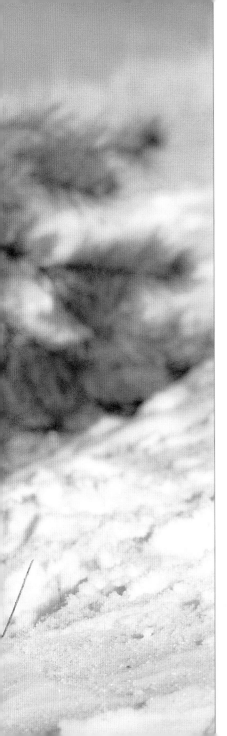

SIBERIAN HUSKY

The Siberian Husky originated in the far north of Russia, where for hundreds of years it was used by the Chukchi people of Siberia for transportation, herding reindeer and guarding, but it is particularly famed for its sled-pulling ability. Whilst it is similar in appearance to other sled dogs, such as the Eskimo Dog and Alaskan Malamute, the Siberian Husky is smaller and much lighter. However, it is no less capable or well adapted to the task than those dogs and, in fact, is much faster, with perhaps even greater stamina. It was these qualities which first aroused interest in the breed outside of its homeland, and in 1909 it was introduced to Alaska, where it proved its worth in a number of long-distance sled-pulling races, in the transportation of furs and medicines, and as an invaluable asset to polar explorers. Essentially a pack animal, the Siberian Husky is also affectionate with people. Although it continues to be employed as a working breed, it is also a popular companion dog.

HEIGHT: 51–61cm (20–24in)
WEIGHT: 16–27kg (35–60lb)
LIFE EXPECTANCY: 12–14 years
COUNTRY OF ORIGIN: Russia
DESCRIPTION: A medium-sized, compact, wolf-like dog, with high-set, erect ears and a fox-like tail. The coat is dense, and colours range from black to pure white, and include greys, browns and reds, often in various combinations

(CANADIAN) ESKIMO DOG

HEIGHT: 50 –69 cm (20–27in)
WEIGHT: 27–48kg (60–105lb)
LIFE EXPECTANCY: 10–12 years
ORIGIN: Canada
DESCRIPTION: A powerful spitz-type dog, with a muscular neck and legs, and a dense, weather-proof coat. The ears are triangular and erect, and the tail carried curled over the back. Colours include black, white, grey, tan and fawn, in a variety of combinations

Also sometimes known as the Husky, the Eskimo Dog is larger and heavier than its Russian counterpart, the Siberian or Arctic Husky, and is also known to be a far more ancient breed, which has been used for hunting and sled pulling by the indigenous Inuit peoples of Canada, Alaska and Greenland for perhaps thousands of years. Well protected from the elements by its dense coat, the Eskimo dog has also long been favoured by polar explorers and surveyors as it possesses incredible strength and stamina. However, the use of skidoos and other dog breeds meant that the Eskimo Dog was almost extinct by about 1970. Despite this setback, with the help of breeders and campaigners, this dog has become increasingly popular in Britain and other parts of Europe in recent years, where it is used in recreational and competitive sledding, and also kept as a companion.

(STANDARD) AMERICAN ESKIMO

A descendant of the German Spitz, which was introduced to the United States by European immigrants, the American Eskimo was first recognized as a distinct breed in 1913, possibly due in part to the tense pre-war political climate. It was renamed four years later, and since that time its own breed standards have been applied. Highly intelligent, loyal and easy to train, the American Eskimo has excelled as a guard dog, in drug detection and in obedience trials, but it was probably first popularized in America as a circus performer with Barnum & Bailey. A member of their American Eskimo troupe, named Stout's Pal Pierre, was the first dog to ever walk a tightrope. This breed is usually affectionate and will typically form a strong and protective bond with its owners, but this may at times make it mistrustful of strangers.

HEIGHT: 38–48cm (14–19in)
WEIGHT: 8–16kg (18–35lb)
LIFE EXPECTANCY: 12–15 years
ORIGIN: USA
DESCRIPTION: A white Spitz-type dog, with a pointed muzzle, erect triangular ears, and a plumed tail, usually carried over its back. The coat is white, sometimes with cream markings, and dense. In males particularly a ruff is often present around the neck

NORWEGIAN ELKHOUND

HEIGHT: 46–53cm
(18–21in)
WEIGHT: 18–27kg
(40–60lb)
LIFE EXPECTANCY: 12–14
years
ORIGIN: Norway
DESCRIPTION: A medium-
sized, squarely built
Spitz-type dog, with
a wedge-shaped
head, erect ears, and
a tail that is curled
tightly over its back.
The coat is dense and
grey, with black on
the muzzle, ears and
tip of tail

Developed for tracking European moose and red deer, both
of which are alternatively referred to as elk, the Norwegian
Elkhound has been known to man since before the Viking
age, and dog skeletons dating from around 5000 BC, which
have been unearthed in caves in Norway, suggest that its
ancestors may have been amongst the earliest of
domesticated breeds. It is still used for hunting, and
demonstrates immense stamina and tenacity as it pursues
its quarry over long distances and treacherous terrain,
before holding it at bay until the arrival of the hunter, and
in addition to large herbivores, the Elkhound has been
successfully employed to hunt rabbits, badgers, wolves,
bears, lynx and mountain lions. It has also been used as a
sled dog, livestock guardian and family companion, and
although it requires a great deal of exercise, its affectionate,
loyal nature makes it a rewarding pet.

FINNISH SPITZ

The national dog of Finland, the Finnish Spitz is descended from ancient hunting dogs, which were introduced to Finland from Central Russia around 2000 years ago, and it continues to be used for hunting to this day. Its principal quarry consists of small mammals like rabbits, hares and squirrels, and game birds such as wood grouse. However, at one time the fearless Finnish Spitz was also employed for hunting much larger game, including bears. Using both scent and sight, it would pursue and corner these large animals, barking to attract the attention of the human hunter. Energetic, hardy and well adapted to working in a cold climate, the Finnish Spitz is also a playful and affectionate breed, and it has become increasingly popular as a family companion. However, on account of its heritage, it requires a great deal of exercise and tends to be highly vocal, in fact it is sometimes also known as the 'barking bird dog'.

HEIGHT: 38–51cm (15–20in)

WEIGHT: 14–16kg (31–35lb)

LIFE EXPECTANCY: 12–14 years

ORIGIN: Finland

DESCRIPTION: A fairly small spitz-type dog, with a pointed muzzle, erect ears and a red to golden coat, which create a fox-like appearance. The tail is plumed, and carried curled over the back

SWEDISH LAPPHUND

Thought to be closely related to the Samoyed of Russia, the Swedish Lapphund is a medium-sized spitz-type dog, and one of two recognized Lapphund breeds, the other being the Finnish Lapphund. Both are thought to share a common ancestry and to have been developed from dogs originally domesticated by the nomadic Lapp, and Sami people in the far north of Europe. Incredibly hardy and with great stamina, these dogs would have proven invaluable in hunting and then herding and guarding the reindeer upon which these people have relied for survival for hundreds of years. It is still used as a herding dog to this day but being highly intelligent, affectionate and responsive to training, it has become increasingly popular as a companion dog, both in its native Sweden and elsewhere. Although not aggressive, the Swedish Lapphund may have a tendency to bark at strangers, but this can usually be reduced by socialization.

HEIGHT: 43–51cm (17–20in)
WEIGHT: 20–21kg (44–47lb)
LIFE EXPECTANCY: 12–14 years
COUNTRY OF ORIGIN: Sweden
DESCRIPTION: A compact, spitz-type dog, with a fox-like face. The ears are triangular and erect, and the tail is carried in a curl over the back. The coat is dense and usually solid black or reddish, but may be bi-coloured with white

SAMOYED

HEIGHT: 48–60cm (19–24in)
WEIGHT: 16–30kg (35–65lb)
LIFE EXPECTANCY: 12–14 years
ORIGIN: Russia
DESCRIPTION: A large, muscular spitz-type dog, with medium-sized, erect ears, and a long tail, which is carried curled over the back. The coat is dense, and may be white, cream or biscuit-coloured

The Samoyed is a large spitz-type dog which originates from the far north of Russia, and takes its name from the ancient Samoyede people of Siberia, a nomadic race of hunters and fishermen who have used this dog for hundreds of years to pull their sleds and herd reindeer. It is a powerful and muscular, yet agile dog, which is ideally suited to the task of sled-pulling, also being protected from the elements by its very dense coat, and it is thought to have been first introduced to Britain in 1889 by the Antarctic explorer Captain Robert Scott, who is amongst several polar explorers to have used the breed for their polar expeditions. Since that time, the elegant and intelligent Samoyed has gone on to become a popular show dog and companion breed, which has an easy-going, sociable nature, but it will typically require patient training when young in order to bring out its best qualities.

NORWEGIAN LUNDEHUND

Also known as the Norwegian Puffin Dog, the Norwegian Lundehund was developed for hunting puffins on steep cliff faces, which has resulted in a number of remarkable characteristics, including additional toes and joints, which aid in climbing and provide increased flexibility, particularly in the neck and shoulders, enabling it to reach into puffin nests where a man could not easily venture. It was employed for hundreds of years in this role until puffins became protected by law during the 1800s, and the Norwegian Lundehund essentially became redundant. As a result, its numbers dwindled, almost to the point of extinction, and despite the efforts of concerned breeders, it remains amongst the rarest of breeds to this day. Intelligent, affectionate and playful, the Norwegian Lundehund makes a good family pet, but it can be shy and somewhat stubborn if not well socialized when young.

HEIGHT: 30–38cm (12–15in)
WEIGHT: 6–9kg (13–20lb)
LIFE EXPECTANCY: 11–13 years
ORIGIN: Norway
DESCRIPTION: A fairly small, spitz-type dog, with a wedge-shaped head, highly mobile, erect ears, and a medium-length tail. The coat is short and rough, and may be reddish-brown with dark hair tips, black or grey, with white markings, or white with black markings. There are six or more toes on each foot

GERMAN SPITZ (MITTEL/STANDARD)

HEIGHT: 30–36cm (12–14in)
WEIGHT: 11–12kg (24–26lb)
LIFE EXPECTANCY: 13–15 years
ORIGIN: Germany
DESCRIPTION: A medium-sized, spitz-type dog, with a profuse coat. The ears are high-set, triangular and erect, and the plumed tail is carried curled over the back. Colours include cream, grey, brown, black, black and white, and black and tan

The Mittel, or Standard, German Spitz is, as its name might suggest, a medium-sized spitz, and is one of four German spitz breeds, which range in size from the Giant German Spitz to the Pomeranian. All are thought to have descended from Nordic herding dogs, such as the Samoyed, and to have been introduced to Germany by the Vikings. They were further refined by crossbreeding with various European herding dogs, and whilst the other members of this group were essentially bred as companions, the Standard German Spitz was commonly employed as a working farm dog. It later found favour as a fashionable companion however, and several were known to have been imported into Britain by Queen Victoria. Generally encountered as a companion breed today, the Standard German Spitz is typically an alert, playful and lively dog, which thrives on human attention.

CHOW CHOW

The Chow Chow is a very ancient and unusual spitz-type dog, and some of its characteristics, such as its blue-black tongue, and the fact that it has 44, rather than the usual 42 teeth (features in common with Central Asian bears), have led to speculation that it may have descended from a prehistoric mammal that both bears and dogs hold as a common ancestor. It has been known to the Chinese for thousands of years, and used for hunting, herding, draught work and guarding, particularly at monasteries, which are thought to have been instrumental in developing selective breeding programmes. The Chow Chow was first taken to the West in the late 18th century, finding popularity with Victorian royalty around 100 years later. Although it can be a wilful and stubborn dog, it can also make an excellent companion if it is well socialized and firmly trained when young.

HEIGHT: 46–56cm (18–22in)
WEIGHT: 20–32kg (45–70lb)
LIFE EXPECTANCY: 12–14 years
ORIGIN: China
DESCRIPTION: A fairly large dog, with a broad head and muzzle. The coat is dense, may be smooth or rough, and red, cinnamon, black or blue in colour. The small ears and ruff behind the head add to the leonine appearance. The tail is usually carried over the back

JAPANESE SPITZ

HEIGHT: 30–36cm (12–14in)
WEIGHT: 5–6kg (11–13lb)
LIFE EXPECTANCY: 10–12 years
ORIGIN: Japan
DESCRIPTION: A white spitz-type dog, with a tapering muzzle, small erect ears and a high-set, plumed tail, that is carried over the back. The coat is short on the lower legs, but long and dense overall

The Japanese Spitz is thought to be directly descended from the much larger Russian Samoyed, although it is often mistaken for the American Eskimo on account of its small size. However, unlike that breed, which was developed more recently from the German Spitz, and which may have cream markings, the Japanese Spitz always possesses a pure white coat. It was specifically bred as a companion dog, and whilst it is highly playful, it is also intelligent, quick to learn and usually obedient. Nevertheless, as with many spitz-type dogs, it tends to be somewhat suspicious of strangers, and may have a tendency to be highly vocal. Whilst this trait may deter some potential owners, it makes the Japanese Spitz a good watchdog, and its generally agreeable temperament has ensured that it has become an increasingly popular pet in both Europe and North America.

(JAPANESE) AKITA

Also known as the Akita Inu, this large spitz is the national dog of Japan, originating from the Akita province on the island of Honshu, where it was once used to hunt bears and other large game as well as being employed as a guard and draught dog. As with all dogs, the Akita was protected by law in Japan during the 18th century, however in the 19th century, an interest in dog fighting was renewed, and this powerful breed suffered heavily as a result. Used for its fur and meat, its numbers were further depleted during the Second World War, bringing this dog almost to the point of extinction. It was rescued by a breeding programme, which was initiated by a Japanese breeder, Mr Ichinoseki. Strong, courageous and extremely loyal, the Akita is used by the police and military in Japan, and its popularity as a companion and guard dog continues to grow in the West.

HEIGHT: 61–71cm (24–28in)
WEIGHT: 34–54kg (75–120lb)
LIFE EXPECTANCY: 10–12 years
ORIGIN: Japan
DESCRIPTION: A muscular spitz-type dog, with a heavy, wedge-shaped head and muzzle. The erect ears are triangular, and the tail is carried over the back. The dense coat may be white, red, cream, brown or blue, often in well-defined combinations, and with a black mask

SPORTING DOGS, GUNDOGS
AND HOUNDS

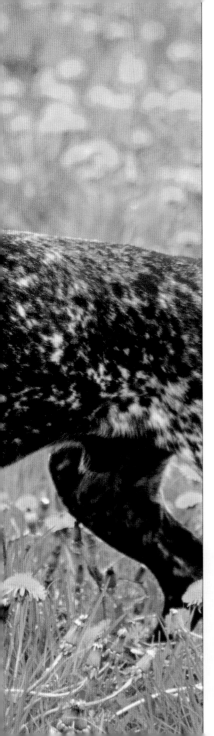

GERMAN SHORT-HAIRED POINTER

The German Short-haired Pointer was developed during the 19th century from various other pointing breeds and hounds, including the English Pointer, in an attempt to produce a more versatile gundog, with increased energy, as well as improved speed, scenting ability and appearance. The result is an allpurpose hunting breed, a dog capable of tracking, pointing and retrieving game, from both land and water. It is most commonly employed in hunting birds such as ducks, pheasants and partridges, but is also used when hunting for rabbits, hares and even deer. Quick to learn and requiring little training, the German Short-haired Pointer also excels in field and obedience trials, and its intelligence and good temperament make it a popular family companion. It is generally healthy, hardy, and relatively long-lived for a dog of this size. However, being highly energetic, it requires a great deal of exercise if it is to remain content, and can otherwise become destructive.

HEIGHT: 53–64cm (21–25in)
WEIGHT: 20–32kg (45–70lb)
LIFE EXPECTANCY: 13–15 years
ORIGIN: Germany
DESCRIPTION: A lean, medium-sized pointer, with a long muzzle, broad, high-set ears, and a tapering tail. The coat is short and dense, and is usually liver or liver and white in colour, and may be patched, ticked or roan

GERMAN WIRE-HAIRED POINTER

Usually larger and more heavily built than the German Short-haired Pointer, the Wire-haired is of similar origins, but it is thought to include the Wire-haired Griffon, Pudelpointer and Stichelhaar, amongst its ancestors, incorporating a variety of pointer, hound and water dog blood. Highly versatile and intelligent as a result, the German Wire-haired Pointer is regarded as a hunt, point and retrieve dog, capable of hunting a diverse range of game over a variety of terrain, and retrieving both on land and from water, its distinctive wiry coat affording it protection from vegetation such as brambles, as well as from cold and wet conditions. Also an excellent companion, the German Wire-haired Pointer is affectionate, loyal and lively, but requires a great deal of exercise in order to remain healthy and content, and can otherwise become wilful and may tend to roam.

HEIGHT: 56–66cm (22–26in)
WEIGHT: 20–34kg (45–75lb)
LIFE EXPECTANCY: 12–14 years
ORIGIN: Germany
DESCRIPTION: A distinctive, wire-coated pointer, with a long, powerful muzzle, beard and moustache. The ears are broad and pendant, and the tail-tip is often docked. The coat may be liver, or liver and white spotted, roan or ticked

WEIMARANER

HEIGHT: 56–69cm (22–27in)
WEIGHT: 22–32kg (48–70lb)
LIFE EXPECTANCY: 11–13 years
ORIGIN: Germany
DESCRIPTION: A fairly large, athletic dog, with a highly distinctive, sleek, grey coat, which has an almost metallic sheen. The ears are moderately long and pendant, and the tail is customarily docked short

Developed in Weimar, in Germany, during the 19th century, the Weimaraner is an all-round hunting dog. It is thought to have resulted from crossbreeding between various scenthounds and pointers, and was first employed to hunt large game such as bears and boar. However, it is capable of hunting, pointing and retrieving, and with the decline of larger game, it was soon in use as a gundog, retrieving small game such as birds. For many years, this breed was unavailable outside Germany, but in the early 20th century it was introduced to Austria and the US and later, to Britain. The Weimaraner is highly active, and requires a great deal of exercise if it is to remain healthy and happy, and it can also be somewhat wilful, but if it is consistently trained when young, it makes a loyal and affectionate companion.

LARGE MÜNSTERLÄNDER

The Large Münsterländer is thought to have been developed from the German Longhaired Pointer during the 1800s, when only liver and white dogs were accepted as the standard for that breed. Regardless of colour, these black and white dogs were obviously still excellent gundogs, and so a separate breed and standard was gradually established, and solidified with the foundation of a breed club in 1919. Intelligent, obedient and hardworking, the Large Münsterländer is capable of tracking, pointing and retrieving, and it is still valued as a hunting companion, whilst its cheerful disposition and devotion to people also ensures that it is an excellent family pet. However, it is likely to be happiest if it can lead an active, outdoor life, and prefers to be close to its owners whenever possible.

HEIGHT: 58–65cm (23–26in)
WEIGHT: 23–32kg (50–70lb)
LIFE EXPECTANCY: 12–14 years
ORIGIN: Germany
DESCRIPTION: A muscular, setter-like dog, with a long, dense coat, with feathering on the chest, ears, legs and tail. The tail is usually carried horizontally, and the ears are broad and pendant. The coat is typically white with black patches, flecking or ticking

BRITTANY (SPANIEL)

Often known simply as the Brittany, in its native France this breed is known as the Épagneul Breton, or the Brittany Spaniel, and it is thought to have been developed in Callac in Brittany during the 1800s, as the result of crossing local spaniels with setters and pointers that had been taken to France by English hunters. An all-round hunting breed, the Brittany is regarded as the only pointing spaniel, and as a hunt, point and retrieve dog that has become probably the most popular gundog in France on account of its versatility. Used for hunting small game, particularly birds such as woodcock, quail and partridge, it has also become highly valued as a hunting companion in the US, and as a popular family pet. It is generally affectionate and easy to look after. However, having been bred as a working dog, the Brittany is highly active and requires a great deal of exercise if it is to remain content, and in order to lessen its desire to roam.

HEIGHT: 43–53cm (17–21in)
WEIGHT: 14–18kg (30–40lb)
LIFE EXPECTANCY: 12–14 years
ORIGIN: France
DESCRIPTION: A medium-sized, compact, but fairly long-legged dog with a slightly feathered coat. The triangular ears are quite high-set, and although the tail is naturally short, it is often docked to around 10cm (4in). Coat colours include orange and white, liver and white, black and white, roan and tri-coloured

ENGLISH SETTER

HEIGHT: 58–69cm (23–27in)
WEIGHT: 20–36kg (45–80lb)
LIFE EXPECTANCY: 12–14 years
ORIGIN: Britain
DESCRIPTION: An elegant setter with a fairly long, square muzzle, long, pendant ears and a tapering tail. The coat is silky, with feathering on the tail, legs and underside, and is white, with blue, lemon, orange or brown speckling

The English Setter is an elegant and responsive breed, which is popular as both a working gundog and show dog, and also as a family companion. It is thought to be descended from old Spanish spaniels, or possibly early water spaniels, pointers and springer spaniel types. Its more recent development is well documented, and the present form of the English Setter is often largely attributed to the efforts of one man, Sir Edward Laverack, who established a breeding programme during the early 19th century. In fact, this dog is still sometimes known as the Laverack Setter today, the word 'setter', being derived from the 'setting' or sitting position adopted when dogs of this kind locate game. Often lively when outdoors, the English Setter is usually placid in the home, although it should still be exercised daily in order to keep it happy and healthy.

GORDON SETTER

Developed in Banffshire in the Scottish Highlands by the fourth Duke of Gordon, the Gordon Setter is somewhat more robust than its English and Irish counterparts, having been selectively bred for increased stamina, and used to hunt, point, flush and retrieve game birds such as grouse on the Scottish moors. The Spanish Pointer and various spaniel breeds are thought to have made up the foundation stock for this breed, with both collies and Bloodhounds contributing to its development; adding to the Gordon Setter's staying power, intelligence and scenting ability, whilst Irish Setter blood was added later, as the breed was refined. A highly popular gundog during the latter part of the 19th century, the breed was in decline by the mid 20th century. However, in recent years it has made something of a recovery, finding favour as a working dog, show dog and family companion.

HEIGHT: 58–68cm (23–27in)
WEIGHT: 22–34kg (48–75lb)
LIFE EXPECTANCY: 10–12 years
ORIGIN: Britain
DESCRIPTION: A fairly tall but robust setter with a deep chest long square muzzle. The ears are long, pendant and slightly pointed, and the tapering tail is well feathered. The silky coat may be straight or wavy, with feathering also on the legs, underside and ears, and is black and tan in colour

IRISH SETTER

Also known as the Irish Red Setter, and perhaps more commonly as the Red Setter, this breed is easily recognized and distinguished from other setters by its luxuriant, chestnut coat. It was developed during the 18th and 19th centuries from a variety of spaniel, setter and pointer breeds, including the Irish Water Spaniel and Gordon Setter, and is an excellent hunting dog, which is most commonly used to point, flush and retrieve game birds, over a variety of terrain. However, in addition to working as a gundog, the Irish Setter has also been used in search and rescue, and as a guide dog for the blind, and is a popular show dog and family companion. On account of its energy and independent nature, the Irish Setter can be slightly more difficult to train than some other setter breeds, and requires a great deal of exercise, but this breed can excel at competitive obedience, and makes a rewarding pet.

HEIGHT: 61–71cm (24–28in)
WEIGHT: 25–34kg (55–75lb)
LIFE EXPECTANCY: 12–14 years
ORIGIN: Ireland
DESCRIPTION: An elegant setter, with a long muzzle, and fairly long, silky, chestnut-coloured coat. The chest, underside, legs and tail are well-feathered, but the hair on the head is short. The ears are long and pendant

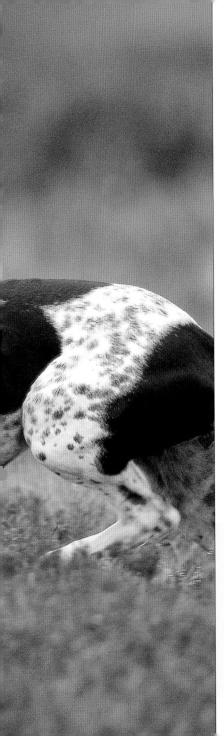

(ENGLISH) POINTER

The English Pointer is thought to be descended from old Spanish or possibly Italian Pointers, which were further developed during the 18th century by crossbreeding with Foxhounds and Greyhounds, in order to increase the breed's stamina and speed. However, setters, the Newfoundland, and even the Bulldog, have also been suggested as contributing to its development. The Pointer takes its name from the stance which it adopts when it has scented game: stopping motionless and pointing in the direction of its quarry with the tail extended, one foreleg raised, and the nose held high. It was first used alongside greyhounds to track and point hares, but was later employed as a gundog, mainly to indicate the position of game birds. Although it typically does not retrieve, the Pointer is still regarded as an excellent hunting dog, and it excels at Pointing Field Trials, but it is also highly popular as a family companion, with a loyal and affectionate disposition.

HEIGHT: 58–66cm (23–26in)
WEIGHT: 20–30kg (44–66lb)
LIFE EXPECTANCY: 12–14 years
ORIGIN: Britain
DESCRIPTION: A large, muscular and athletic pointer, with a long, square muzzle. The ears are pendant and medium-sized, and the tail is straight and tapering. The coat is short and sleek, and is usually mainly white, but may be liver, lemon, black or reddish, and solid, patched or speckled

AMERICAN COCKER SPANIEL

The American Cocker Spaniel was developed from English Cocker Spaniels that were exported to North America during the 19th century, and whilst initially it differed only in size, having been bred to be smaller, by 1945 it differed significantly enough to be recognized as a breed in its own right. The American Cocker Spaniel shares several characteristics with its larger cousin, but has a thicker, more luxuriant coat, resulting in a more heavily feathered abdomen, ears and legs. Lively and playful, this breed is a popular family pet, but it is also used for hunting and retrieving. In fact, the Cocker Spaniel was traditionally used for the flushing and retrieval of game birds, particularly quail and woodcock, and it is from this bird that the name 'Cocker' is derived.

HEIGHT: 36–38cm (14–15in)
WEIGHT: 10–14kg (22–31lb)
LIFE EXPECTANCY: 12–15 years
ORIGIN: USA
DESCRIPTION: A small, compact spaniel, with a rounded head, broad muzzle, long hanging ears, and a fairly long, silky coat. Coat may be a solid colour, black-and-tan, or a variation of white with black, buff or red, or white with black and tan points. The tail is typically docked

(ENGLISH) COCKER SPANIEL

HEIGHT: 38–41cm (14–16in)
WEIGHT: 12–15kg (26–33lb)
LIFE EXPECTANCY: 12–14 years
ORIGIN: Britain
DESCRIPTION: A fairly small, compact spaniel, with long ears and a medium-length coat. The underside and legs are feathered, and the tail is often docked quite short. Colours include black, liver and red, roan, and white with black, liver or red markings

Whilst spaniels have been known since the 14th century, it was not until hundreds of years later that they began to be differentiated according to the various tasks that they were being developed to perform; be it flushing or springing game, retrieving from water or in the case of the English Cocker Spaniel, flushing woodcock. Still popular as a gundog, this breed has also become highly regarded as a family companion, no doubt on account of its sociable and affectionate disposition. The Cocker Spaniel is also relatively easy to train, and tends to perform well at both agility and obedience trials. It enjoys swimming and roaming off the lead, but care should always be taken to maintain its coat, prevent matting and remove any plant seeds and other debris, as the Cocker Spaniel can be quite prone to infections of the eyes and ears.

FIELD SPANIEL

Developed alongside the English Cocker Spaniel, the larger and heavier Field Spaniel was recognized as a distinct breed in the latter half of the 19th century, but soon afterwards, its existence was threatened by poor breeding practices, which involved crossbreeding with the Sussex Spaniel. This resulted in a longer, heavier dog, which proved to be less effective in the field. The Field Spaniel was restored to its former, more moderate type, and began to be seen once more at work and in the show ring. It has never really achieved the popularity of either the English Cocker or Springer Spaniels, although it is widely considered to combine the best attributes of those dogs, with one of the mildest temperaments of any spaniel. As such, it makes an excellent family pet, but it is also a capable gundog.

HEIGHT: 43–46cm (17–18in)
WEIGHT: 18–25kg (40–55lb)
LIFE EXPECTANCY: 10–12 years
ORIGIN: Britain
DESCRIPTION: A medium-sized, long-bodied spaniel, with long, feathered ears, and a silky coat, which is usually brown or black, sometimes with tan markings, or may be roan. The legs, chest, underside and tail are feathered, but the tail is usually docked short

ENGLISH SPRINGER SPANIEL

Thought to be the ancestor of most other British spaniels, and amongst the oldest of the British gundogs, the English Springer Spaniel was in fact used for flushing or 'springing' game into nets, long before guns were developed for use in hunting. However, it is also an excellent retriever, and remains popular as a working dog. It was recognized by the British Kennel Club as a distinct breed in 1902, with the first spaniel field trials being held three years later, since which time, two forms have emerged, with show dogs typically being taller and more lightly built than their working counterparts. Additionally, the English Springer Spaniel is well admired as an intelligent, affectionate and sociable family pet, and it has also been successfully employed by various police and security forces as a sniffer dog.

HEIGHT: 46–56cm (18–21in)
WEIGHT: 18–25kg (40–55lb)
LIFE EXPECTANCY: 12–14 years
ORIGIN: Britain
DESCRIPTION: A medium-sized, compact dog, with long pendant ears. The medium-length, feathered coat may be liver and white, black and white, sometimes with tan markings, blue or liver roan. The tail is generally docked

WELSH SPRINGER SPANIEL

HEIGHT: 41–48cm
(16–19in)
WEIGHT: 16–20kg
(35–45lb)
LIFE EXPECTANCY: 12–14
years
ORIGIN: Britain
DESCRIPTION: A compact,
medium-sized spaniel,
with a silky, medium-
length, dark red and
white coat, which may
be is straight or slightly
wavy, and has
feathering on the chest,
undersides, legs, ears
and tail. The ears are
quite long and pendant,
and the tail is
sometimes docked

Although regarded as a fairly ancient breed, which may
have developed from the same French spaniel stock as
the Brittany, the Welsh Springer Spaniel was relatively
unknown outside Wales until the end of the 19th
century, and was originally known as the Welsh Cocker
Spaniel until it was officially recognized by the British
Kennel Club in 1902, and its name was formally
changed. A highly capable, hardworking gundog, its
name is derived from its hunting style, whereby it will
'spring' game from cover, but it is also an excellent
retriever that will work in inhospitable conditions over
difficult terrain, and in addition, makes a loyal and
affectionate companion. The Welsh Springer Spaniel is
similar in appearance to its English counterpart, but it
is smaller and more lightly built, with distinctive, rich
red markings on its white coat.

CLUMBER SPANIEL

The Clumber Spaniel, which is the heaviest of the spaniel breeds, is named after Clumber Park in Nottinghamshire, where the second Duke of Newcastle developed the breed in the late 18th and early 19th centuries. However, it is thought that the original stock may have been introduced from France during the French Revolution. Favoured by English royalty, the Clumber Spaniel was originally used to track, flush and retrieve game birds such as pheasant and partridge from dense undergrowth, later becoming admired as a show dog. Although it has never achieved the popularity of many other spaniel breeds, either in the show ring or working in the field, its affectionate nature and even temperament make it an ideal family companion. When working, the Clumber Spaniel tends to be slower than other gundogs on account of its size, but it is still also used in that role.

HEIGHT: 41–51cm (16–20in)
WEIGHT: 25–39kg (55–85lb)
LIFE EXPECTANCY: 10–12 years
ORIGIN: Britain
DESCRIPTION: A large, heavily built spaniel, with a deep, broad chest, and relatively short legs. The eyes are quite deeply set, the ears are large and the tail is usually docked. The coat is feathered, and white, with orange or lemon markings

IRISH WATER SPANIEL

HEIGHT: 53–61cm
(21–24in)
WEIGHT: 20–29kg
(45–65lb)
LIFE EXPECTANCY: 10–12
years
ORIGIN: Ireland
DESCRIPTION: A tall
spaniel, with a highly
distinctive, tightly
curled coat, which is
liver in colour, with a
purple tint. The ears are
long, oval and pendant,
and the tail is short,
and may be hairless, or
covered in short,
straight hair

A large and distinctive spaniel, the Irish Water Spaniel was developed in Ireland during the 1800s by Mr Justin McCarthy, who, somewhat intriguingly, never revealed the breed's ancestry. However, it seems likely that Portuguese Water Dogs, Poodles and Irish spaniels were influential in its development. It was bred specifically for hunting and retrieving waterfowl, such as snipe, ducks and geese, and is a powerful swimmer with a natural affinity for water and an oily, water-resistant coat, but it is also a proficient retriever on land. Highly intelligent and loyal, the Irish Water Spaniel is also an excellent companion and watchdog, which will form a strong bond with its owners, although it should be well trained and socialized when young in order to prevent it from becoming too wary of strangers. This breed also requires plenty of exercise, and will welcome the opportunity to swim and retrieve.

PORTUGUESE WATER DOG

Although regarded as a gundog due to its excellent retrieving abilities, for hundreds of years this breed was used by Portuguese fishermen for a variety of tasks, including the retrieval of nets, tackle or other items that had been lost overboard, carrying messages between boats and to the shore, and also as a guard dog when the boats were in harbour. With technological advances, the Portuguese Water Dog became increasingly redundant and had almost died out by around the 1930s, but its fortunes were reversed with the aid of breeding programmes designed to save the dog from extinction. The breed is now established in a number of countries. Today the Portuguese Water Dog is mainly a companion, but as it is intelligent and easily trained with an excellent temperament, it is also used as a therapy and assistance dog.

HEIGHT: 43–53cm (17–23in)
WEIGHT: 16–25kg (35–55lb)
LIFE EXPECTANCY: 11–13 years
ORIGIN: Portugal
DESCRIPTION: A muscular, medium-sized dog, with a large head, heart-shaped, pendant ears and a tapering tail. The coat may be wavy or tightly curled, and either cut in a lion clip, or cropped fairly short overall. Coat colours include black, white and brown

STANDARD POODLE

Although all three varieties of Poodle are sometimes grouped together as working or utility dogs, or alternatively, simply as companion breeds, the Standard Poodle, which is the forebear of the Miniature and Toy forms, was essentially developed as a water dog, that is, as a gundog that would readily retrieve game from water, and the traditional continental-clip was originally intended to lighten the weight of the coat for swimming, whilst protecting the major organs and joints from the cold. Today the Standard Poodle retains a keen hunting instinct, and has even been used to forage for truffles, but it is most commonly found as a family pet. Interestingly, there remains some controversy over its origins, for whilst France has claimed it as its own, and is certainly where the breed was miniaturized, the Standard Poodle is often accepted as having been developed in Germany, albeit at least in part from a French dog, the Barbet.

HEIGHT: 38–76cm (15–30in)
WEIGHT: 20–35kg (45–77lb)
LIFE EXPECTANCY: 12–14 years
ORIGIN: Germany
DESCRIPTION: A medium-sized to large, athletic dog, with a long, straight muzzle, broad, pendant ears, and a high-set tail, which is typically docked by half. The coat is profuse, wiry and curly, and is often clipped short overall, or the rear half of the body, upper legs and tail are shaved. It occurs in a wide range of solid colours

GOLDEN RETRIEVER

Thought to be the result of crossbreeding between a yellow Flat-coated Retriever, and the now extinct Tweed Water Spaniel, the Golden Retriever originated in Britain during the 1860s, where for many years it was known as the Golden Flat-coat. The breed was further developed by the introduction of Labrador, Irish Setter and Bloodhound stock, to produce an excellent hunting companion, with a keen sense of smell, and the ability to retrieve game birds from both land and water. Intelligent and easily trained, with an affectionate disposition, the Golden Retriever is still used as a gundog, and excels in field and obedience trials. However, it is also widely used as a therapy dog, a guide dog for the blind, and is employed in drugs detection by police forces and customs officials. Additionally, it has become one of the most popular of all family companion breeds.

HEIGHT: 51–61cm (20–24in)
WEIGHT: 25–36kg (55–80lb)
LIFE EXPECTANCY: 10–12 years
ORIGIN: Britain
DESCRIPTION: A distinctive retriever, with a broad head and muzzle, medium-sized, pendant ears, and a long, well-feathered tail. The coat is of medium length, with feathering also present on the chest and legs, and is cream to golden in colour

FLAT-COATED RETRIEVER

HEIGHT: 55–58cm (22–23in)
WEIGHT: 27–32kg (60–70lb)
LIFE EXPECTANCY: 10–12 years
ORIGIN: Britain
DESCRIPTION: A medium-sized, muscular retriever, with a fairly long head and wide muzzle. The medium-length coat is thick and fine, but lies flat to the body, with feathering on the legs, tail and chest. It may be black or liver in colour

Although originating in Britain, two Canadian breeds, the Labrador Retriever and the Newfoundland, were the major contributors to its development, probably with the addition of Irish Setter, spaniel and sheepdog stock, whilst Mr S. E. Shirley, the founder of the UK Kennel Club is considered instrumental in its refinement. An excellent gundog, with intelligence, stamina and a fine nose, the Flat-coated Retriever was used to locate and retrieve game in a variety of conditions, including densely vegetated terrain and water. It became highly popular during the early 20th century, although by the end of the Second World War, its popularity had waned. However, to this day, the Flat-coated Retriever maintains a dedicated following of enthusiasts, and continues to prove itself as a working, show and companion dog of exceptional quality.

CHESAPEAKE BAY RETRIEVER

The story of the Chesapeake Bay Retriever is thought to begin in 1807, when an English ship carrying two Newfoundland pups got into difficulty off the coast of Maryland. These dogs were rescued and presented as a gift to the local sailors. These dogs, and their progeny, were subsequently bred with retrievers and hunting dogs, such as Flat- and Curly-coated Retrievers, the Irish Water Spaniel, Otter Hounds and coonhounds, resulting in excellent tracking and retrieving dogs, which had a natural affinity for water, high levels of stamina, and dense, oily, protective coats. By 1885, a breed standard had been established, and the Chesapeake Bay Retriever was recognized as a breed in its own right. Today it is probably without equal as a retriever, particularly when working in water, and it makes a fine family pet if well trained, socialized and given plenty of exercise.

HEIGHT: 53–66cm (21–26in)
WEIGHT: 25–36kg (55–80lb)
LIFE EXPECTANCY: 10–12 years
ORIGIN: USA
DESCRIPTION: A muscular retriever, with a broad head, powerful muzzle, and slightly feathered tail. The coat is dense and occurs in various shades of brown, often with white markings on the chest and feet

LABRADOR RETRIEVER

Also sometimes known as the Saint John's Dog, the Labrador Retriever originated in Newfoundland in Canada, where it was first employed to haul fishermen's nets ashore, before later becoming popular as a gundog, and particularly as a retriever of waterfowl, a role which it is still found in to this day. This highly intelligent, easily trained breed is also commonly found as a sniffer dog, guide dog for the blind and therapy dog, and on account of its gentle, calm and affectionate nature, it has become one of the most popular of family companions on both sides of the Atlantic. Although the Labrador Retriever is of Canadian origin, a distinction is often made between dogs of North American and British Stock, with the latter typically being more heavily built, and the former, slightly taller. In both cases, however, regular exercise is required in order to prevent them from becoming overweight.

HEIGHT: 53–61cm (21–24in)
WEIGHT: 25–34kg (55–75lb)
LIFE EXPECTANCY: 10–12 years
ORIGIN: Canada
DESCRIPTION: A solid, slightly elongated, muscular retriever, with a broad head, medium-sized pendant ears and a tapering, otter-like tail. The coat is short, hard and straight, and may be black, yellow or chocolate in colour

CURLY-COATED RETRIEVER

The Curly-coated Retriever is thought to be amongst the oldest of the retrievers, although several old breeds are thought to have contributed to its development, including the Close-curled English Water Dog, Old Water Spaniel, St John's Newfoundland dog, the Retrieving Setter and possibly the Labrador and Poodle. An outstanding gundog, it was favoured by gamekeepers during the 18th century for its intelligence and stamina, and although today its loyalty, affection and obedience have increased its popularity as a family companion, it continues to be used for hunting and retrieving, and it is also employed as a therapy dog. Highly energetic, with a love of water, the Curly-coated Retriever requires plenty of physical and mental stimulation if it is to remain content, and it should be well socialized when young, in order to prevent it from becoming overcautious with strangers and other dogs when it is older.

HEIGHT: 61–68cm (24–27in)
WEIGHT: 30–36kg (66–80lb)
LIFE EXPECTANCY: 8–12 years
ORIGIN: Britain
DESCRIPTION: A large retriever with a wedge-shaped head and tapering muzzle. The distinctive black or liver coloured coat is tightly curled overall, but smooth on the face. The tail tapers and is typically carried straight

NOVA SCOTIA DUCK-TOLLING RETRIEVER

HEIGHT: 46–53cm (18–21in)
WEIGHT: 17–21kg (37–51lb)
LIFE EXPECTANCY: 12–14 years
ORIGIN: Canada
DESCRIPTION: A small but muscular retriever, with high-set, pendant ears, and a feathered tail. The coat is quite long and dense, and is reddish or orange in colour, sometimes with white markings on the feet, chest and tail

As its name suggests, the Nova Scotia Duck-tolling Retriever was developed in Nova Scotia, and was used to toll, or lure, waterfowl within the range of hunters' guns, before retrieving the birds from the water once they had been shot. The dog creates a disturbance at the shoreline which lures the inquisitive ducks or geese, much in the manner that foxes sometimes do, although it is often encouraged to do so by retrieving a ball or stick thrown by the hunter from a concealed position. The smallest of the retrievers, this breed is powerful, hardworking and agile, and is perhaps best kept as a working dog on account of its high energy levels and desire to retrieve, but if it otherwise receives plenty of exercise and the opportunity to swim, it makes an excellent companion breed, which is usually good with both people and other dogs.

RHODESIAN RIDGEBACK

Originating from South African hunting dogs, this powerful hound is named after the country where its breed standard was fixed in 1922, Rhodesia (now Zimbabwe), and for the ridge of hair that runs along the length of its back. A combination of sight and scenthound, the Rhodesian Ridgeback was once employed for hunting big game and it is sometimes alternatively known as the African Lion Dog, but it has also been used to hunt smaller quarry, as a retrieving gundog, a guard dog, and even for racing. The attempts to train this breed for police use have proven largely unsuccessful due to the repetitive nature of such training. Highly intelligent, affectionate and loyal, it is also popular as a companion, but requires thorough obedience training, and socialization with people and other dogs.

HEIGHT: 61–67cm (24–26in)
WEIGHT: 30–39kg (66–86lb)
LIFE EXPECTANCY: 10–12 years
ORIGIN: South Africa
DESCRIPTION: A large, muscular hound with a broad skull and powerful muzzle. The ears are heart-shaped and pendant, the tail strong and tapering. The coat is short and sleek, with a distinctive ridge of hair along the back, and is wheaten in colour, sometimes with white markings on the chest and feet

DALMATIAN

Popularized by the Dodie Smith
book *The Hundred and One
Dalmatians*, and the Walt Disney film
that was based on it, the Dalmatian is
probably one of the most instantly
recognizable of breeds, identifiable
by its starkly contrasting white and
black-spotted coat. It has been
known since at least the 1400s but
its exact origins are uncertain, and
debate continues as to whether it is
of Eastern European, Asian or
African origin. What is known is that
by the 1800s, the Dalmatian had
become popular as a carriage and
stable dog in Europe, running
alongside horse-drawn coaches to act
as a deterrent and guard dog against
would-be robbers, and controlling
vermin in the stables. It was also
employed in a similar role when fire
equipment was horse-drawn, and
remains familiar as a mascot of the
fire services. Today the Dalmatian is
popular as a companion breed, but,
as its history might suggest, it is
highly energetic and requires a great
deal of exercise.

HEIGHT: 50–60cm (20–24in)
WEIGHT: 18–27kg (40–60lb)
LIFE EXPECTANCY: 10–12 years
ORIGIN: Croatia
DESCRIPTION: A lean but muscular dog, with a
   sleek, black or liver-spotted coat. The ears
   are high-set and pendant, and the tail
   quite long and tapering. Puppies are born
   white, with the spots developing later

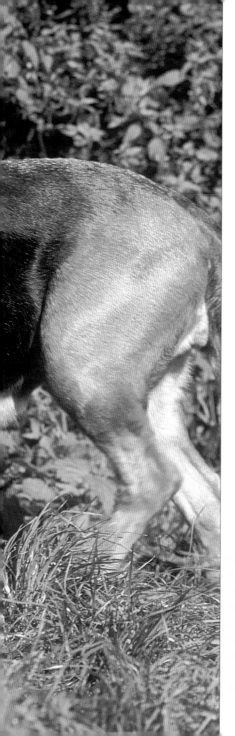

BLOODHOUND

Occasionally still known as the St Hubert Hound, the Bloodhound is amongst the oldest of dog breeds, and its origins can be traced back as far as the Belgian monastery established by St Hubert, the patron saint of hunting, during the 7th century. It was brought to England around the time of the Norman Conquest, and it is thought to be an ancestor of almost all the scenthound breeds that were developed in Britain. Best known for its incredible tracking ability, the Bloodhound was originally used to hunt wild animals, such as foxes and deer, but being able to pick up and follow a scent which is several days old, over a course of 200 kilometres (124 miles) or more, it has been used in search and rescue work, and by the police to pursue criminals. The Bloodhound makes a gentle and affectionate companion, but it can be wilful at times, particularly if distracted by an interesting scent, and it also has a tendency to drool, snore and howl.

HEIGHT: 58–69cm (23–27in)
WEIGHT: 36–50kg (80–110lb)
LIFE EXPECTANCY: 10–12 years
ORIGIN: Belgium
DESCRIPTION: A huge, powerful hound, with a long muzzle, drooping ears, loose, wrinkled skin and a conspicuous dewlap. The coat is short, and black and tan, liver and tan, or red

OTTER HOUND/OTTERHOUND

HEIGHT: 61–69cm (24–27in)

WEIGHT: 30–52kg (66–115lb)

LIFE EXPECTANCY: 10–12 years

ORIGIN: Britain

DESCRIPTION: A large, rough-coated hound, with a large head with shaggy facial hair, and a muscular neck with an abundant dewlap. The ears are long and pendulous, and the tail is often carried with an upward curve. The coat is usually grizzle or wheaten with black markings

As its name would suggest, the Otter Hound was bred specifically for hunting otters, and whilst it is known to have been developed in Britain from at least as far back as the 14th century, its precise origins are somewhat unclear. However, it is thought that it may have evolved from a combination of early foxhounds, French griffons, the Bloodhound, and English rough-haired terriers. For hundreds of years it was used as a pack-hound, employed to protect fish stocks in lakes and rivers from predation by otters, but with the decline in numbers of its quarry, by the 20th century the Otter Hound's usefulness and popularity had diminished severely. The breed was rescued by the concerted efforts of several breeders, and began to be found both in the show ring and as a companion breed. In the US it has also been employed to hunt mink, raccoons and even bears.

(ENGLISH) FOXHOUND

A solid, muscular scenthound, the English Foxhound is built for stamina, strength and short bursts of speed, having been developed to hunt in packs for foxes, accompanied by horses and riders. Various breeds are thought to have contributed to the Foxhound's make-up, from the French St Hubert Hound to the Greyhound, Fox Terrier, and even the Bulldog, resulting in a highly active dog that has an excellent nose for a scent; traits that should be taken into account when considering the Foxhound as a family pet. This breed can make a fine companion, but it requires plenty of exercise on a daily basis if it is to remain content, and may otherwise become destructive or begin to roam. Whilst the Foxhound is generally responsive and friendly, it should also be remembered that it is essentially a pack dog, and enjoys, if not requires, the company of its own kind.

HEIGHT: 53–63cm (21–25in)
WEIGHT: 25–32kg (55–70lb)
LIFE EXPECTANCY: 10–12 years
ORIGIN: Britain
DESCRIPTION: A muscular, yet elegant hound, with a long neck and muzzle, and strong hindquarters. The ears are long and pendant, the tail long and tapering. The coat is short, and typically tri-coloured in black, white and tan

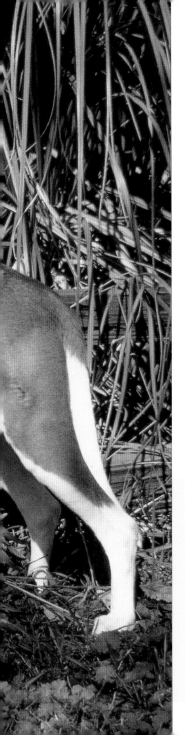

AMERICAN FOXHOUND

Developed during the 1700s, the American Foxhound is descended from English Foxhounds that were taken to the US in the 1650s, the progeny of which were later crossbred with hounds that had been sent to George Washington by the French general Lafayette. Highly similar to the English Foxhound, this breed was, however, developed to be lighter-boned and quicker of pace, with a keener sense of smell and greater stamina; overall, better suited to the rolling countryside of Virginia and Maryland. The American Foxhound was, and continues to be, used for hunting foxes, and a variety of other small game, both in packs and alone, but is perhaps slightly better suited to life as a companion than its English counterpart, which has traditionally been almost exclusively kennelled in packs. It is affectionate by nature, with a melodious voice, but requires a great deal of exercise, and will tend to roam if it picks up an interesting scent.

HEIGHT: 53–64cm (21–25in)
WEIGHT: 30–34kg (65–75lb)
LIFE EXPECTANCY: 10–12 years
ORIGIN: USA
DESCRIPTION: A large, athletic scenthound, with a long muzzle, broad pendant ears, and a fairly long tail, which is carried in an upward curve. The coat is short and hard, and usually tri-coloured in white and tan, with a black saddle

(LOUISIANA) CATAHOULA LEOPARD DOG

Named for its spotted or mottled coat, and the area of Catahoula in Louisiana, where it is thought to have originated, and where it is now the state dog, the Catahoula Leopard Dog is a muscular and versatile hound that has been used in hunting, herding, drug detection, search and rescue, and as a loyal guard and watchdog. With its heavily-webbed feet, it has been used extensively to round cattle and pigs from marshy terrain, as well as for hunting boar, and it is sometimes also known as the Catahoula Hog Dog. Its exact origins are uncertain, but it has been suggested that it may have developed as hybrids between mastiffs, which were taken to the Americas during the early Spanish exploration of the New World, and native Red Wolves, which were later crossed with the Beauceron by French explorers.

HEIGHT: 51–66cm (20–26in)
WEIGHT: 23–36kg (50–80lb)
LIFE EXPECTANCY: 12–14 years
ORIGIN: USA
DESCRIPTION: A compact, muscular hound, with a deep chest, long tapering tail and pendant triangular ears. The coat is short, and merle or black and tan. It is common for the eyes of an individual to differ in colour

HARRIER/HAREHOUND

HEIGHT: 48–56cm
(19–22in)
WEIGHT: 18–27kg
(40–60lb)
LIFE EXPECTANCY: 10–12
years
ORIGIN: Britain
DESCRIPTION: A compact,
muscular hound, with a
deep chest, broad head
and square muzzle. The
ears are rounded and
pendant, the tail of
medium length and
carried high. The coat is
short and hard, and is
usually white with
lemon, red or tan,
often with a black
saddle

Similar in appearance to the English Foxhound, it is
thought that the Harrier, or Harehound, was developed
from the Foxhound, Greyhound and Fox Terrier,
although some sources also cite the Bloodhound and
Basset Hound as having contributed to its development.
Originating as a scenting pack hound in the 1200s, the
Harrier is smaller and more compact than the Foxhound,
and was employed primarily to hunt hares, accompanied
by hunters on foot, but it has also been used in
foxhunting. The Harrier has an exceptional sense of smell
and great stamina, making it an excellent working dog,
but it is also a good companion breed, being more
playful, extrovert and at home with human company than
the Foxhound. Having been developed as a pack animal,
this breed is also usually sociable with other dogs, but it
may be aggressive towards cats and other small animals,
unless it has been raised with them.

BASSET HOUND

The name basset is derived from the French word 'bas' meaning low, and describes the low-set build of several breeds. However, the Basset Hound was actually produced in Britain, from a combination of French and Belgian bassets crossed with the Bloodhound. It was developed as a hunting dog, used to track game such as deer, foxes, rabbits and hares, and like the Bloodhound, it has an exceptional sense of smell and great stamina, but on account of its short legs and weight, it is amongst the slowest of all the hounds. In fact, this breed is heavier-boned in relation to its size than any other dog, and can develop problems with its legs if it is allowed to become obese. It should therefore never be overfed, and be exercised regularly. A rewarding, devoted family pet, with a deep, melodious voice, the Basset Hound can be stubborn at times, particularly if it has picked up an interesting scent.

HEIGHT: 28–38cm (11–15in)
WEIGHT: 18–27kg (40–60lb)
LIFE EXPECTANCY: 10–12 years
ORIGIN: Britain
DESCRIPTION: A long and low-set hound, with a deep chest, large head, very long, velvety ears, and a pronounced dewlap. The coat is short and shiny, and is usually black, tan and white in colour

BEAGLE

Thought to be descended from the English Foxhound and possibly the Harrier, the Beagle is amongst the oldest of British hounds, and probably originated around the 1300s. It is a small scenthound, which was traditionally used to hunt rabbits and hares, as well as game birds. Whilst it remains a popular hunting dog, on account of its intelligence, stamina and calm disposition, today it is commonly kept as a family pet, and owing to its keen sense of smell, is often also employed as a police sniffer dog. As a pet, this breed is affectionate and playful, but it is also independent and inquisitive, and may display a tendency to roam. If left alone for a long period of time, a Beagle will often attempt to escape, failing which, it may howl incessantly. However, this kind of behaviour may be checked if the dog is appropriately trained from a young age, or if it is kept with a companion.

HEIGHT: 33–41cm (13–16in)
WEIGHT: 8–14kg (18–30lb)
LIFE EXPECTANCY: 12–15 years
ORIGIN: Britain
DESCRIPTION: A small, sturdy hound, with a broad head and square muzzle. The ears are long and pendant, the coat short and most commonly black, tan and white in colour

DACHSHUND

HEIGHT: 20–28cm (8–11in)
WEIGHT: 5–12kg (11–26lb)
LIFE EXPECTANCY: 11–13 years
ORIGIN: Germany
DESCRIPTION: An elongated,
muscular dog, with short
legs, and a long head
and muzzle. The ears are
pendant but mobile, and
the tail is relatively long.
The coat may be short,
long or wiry, and colours
and markings include
black, tan, chestnut, grey,
piebald, speckled or
harlequin

The Dachshund is a short-legged hound, with an
elongated body, which occurs in two forms: standard
and miniature, both of which are found in three coat
varieties: smooth, wire, and long-haired. All combine
qualities of both hounds and terriers, being keen
diggers with excellent scenting ability, good stamina
and tenacity, and they were originally used to track
small mammals, before digging or flushing them from
their burrows. Whilst the standard Dachshund was
used to hunt badgers, the smaller form was developed
to catch rabbits, stoats and rodents. Today the
Dachshund is most commonly found as a companion,
and being intelligent, inquisitive and playful, it makes a
good family pet. However, it can experience spinal
problems, and should be discouraged from jumping or
otherwise overexerting itself.

AFGHAN HOUND

Although the exact history of the Afghan Hound is uncertain, it is known to be of ancient descent, probably originating from Salukis brought from Syria into Afghanistan, where the extremes of temperature may have prompted the development of a thicker coat. Highly intelligent, fast and agile, it was used as both a shepherding and hunting dog, pursuing wild goats, ibex, gazelle, and even wolves and snow leopards. The purity of the breed was maintained by its isolation in the mountains of Afghanistan, and it was not introduced to Great Britain until the early 1900s by soldiers returning from military campaigns. It prompted a sensation after being exhibited as an 'Oriental Greyhound' in 1907 at the Crystal Palace exhibition, going on to become a popular pet and symbol of luxury and aristocracy. Today the species may also be found in use as a tracking and racing breed.

HEIGHT: 66–74cm (26–29in)
WEIGHT: 23–34kg (52–64lb)
LIFE EXPECTANCY: 12–14 years
ORIGIN: Afghanistan
DESCRIPTION: A tall, slender and elegant hound, with a long head, neck and ears. The coat is typically long, silky and sandy-coloured overall, shorter and darker on the face, but darker, lighter and brindle or spotted individuals are not uncommon

BORZOI

HEIGHT: 66–79cm (26–31in)
WEIGHT: 27–48kg (60–105lb)
LIFE EXPECTANCY: 10–12 years
ORIGIN: Russia
DESCRIPTION: A tall and elegant hound, with a narrow head and long muzzle. The ears are usually swept back, and the coat is of medium length, with feathering on the legs, underside and long, curving tail. Colours include white, golden, tan and grey, which may be solid or mixed

Also known as the Russian Wolfhound, this fast and graceful hound originated in Russia, where it was once used to hunt wolves, and its name is derived from a Russian word meaning swift. It is thought to have descended from ancient greyhound-types, such as the Saluki, probably crossed with long-haired herding dogs, and was a popular hunting dog with the Russian nobility, and later as a companion to royalty and the aristocracy throughout much of Europe. Both Queen Victoria and Princess Alexandra were presented with Borzois as gifts. Since being shown in 1891 at the first Crufts Dog Show, this breed has won numerous competition titles. A popular show dog and family pet to this day, the Borzoi is an attractive, intelligent and affectionate companion, but whilst usually calm and peaceful indoors, it requires a great deal of exercise and the space to run freely.

SALUKI

Named after the old Arabian city of Saluk, the Saluki is of very ancient origin, and dogs of a similar type were known to the ancient Egyptians, as is evidenced by the discovery of images in Egyptian tombs, and even the mummified remains of dogs. A fast and agile sighthound, sometimes known as the Gazelle Hound, it was originally used to hunt gazelles, foxes, jackals and hares in the inhospitable desert, probably in conjunction with hunting falcons. Since its introduction to the West, this breed has mainly been a companion and show dog, but it has also been used for racing. The Saluki is usually a calm and affectionate pet, but it retains a strong hunting instinct. It requires plenty of exercise. Care should be taken if it is allowed off the leash, as it will pursue any small animals it sees, with no heed to its owner's calls.

HEIGHT: 43–71cm (17–28in)
WEIGHT: 16–29kg (35–65lb)
LIFE EXPECTANCY: 11–13 years
ORIGIN: Middle East
DESCRIPTION: A very athletic, elegant hound, with a narrow, tapering head and long, pendant ears. The coat is short overall, with long, silky feathering on the ears and tail. Coat colours include black and tan, fawn, white, cream and red, also in various combinations

(SCOTTISH)
DEERHOUND

Sometimes mistaken for the Irish
Wolfhound on account of its size
and wiry coat, the Deerhound is
more slender and less powerfully
built, with a more elongated
muzzle. It is an ancient breed,
which is descended from the
greyhound, and as its name
suggests, it was developed in
Scotland in order to hunt deer. Also
known as the Royal Dog of
Scotland, it was the favoured
hunting dog of the Scottish nobility
for many years, until the advent of
guns effectively rendered it
superfluous. However, interest in
the breed was revived during the
19th century, and it was saved from
the possible threat of extinction.
Although still not common today,
the Deerhound is employed in
hunting and tracking, is used in
sporting activities such as racing
and lure coursing, and is kept as a
show dog and family pet.

HEIGHT: 71–81cm (28–32in)
WEIGHT: 34–50kg (75–110lb)
LIFE EXPECTANCY: 10–12 years
ORIGIN: Britain
DESCRIPTION: A tall, slim hound, with a
tapering muzzle, very long tail, and small
ears, which are usually folded back
against the head. The coat is harsh and
shaggy, and usually grey in colour,
although sandy, red and brindle also
occur

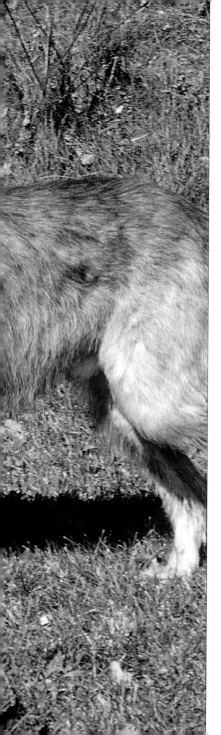

IRISH WOLFHOUND

The Irish Wolfhound is one of the tallest dogs in the world, and although it is also heavy and muscular, it retains the elegance of the Greyhound, from which it is thought to have developed. An ancient hunting breed, it was used in the pursuit of wolves, boar and elk by the Irish nobility for hundreds of years, and was also exported to England on royal request. However, once the wolf had been hunted to the brink of extinction in Britain and Ireland during the 18th and 19th centuries, Irish Wolfhound numbers also declined severely. It was re-established during the late 19th century, mainly due to the efforts of one man, a Scottish army officer, Captain George Graham, who is thought to have crossbred surviving Irish Wolfhounds with the Deerhound, Great Dane and the Borzoi, in order to rescue the breed. Despite its imposing appearance, the Irish Wolfhound is a gentle and affectionate dog, which is typically inactive indoors, but like other sighthounds it will enjoy running freely whenever possible.

HEIGHT: 71–90cm (28–35in)
WEIGHT: 40–69kg (90–150lb)
LIFE EXPECTANCY: 8–10 years
ORIGIN: Ireland
DESCRIPTION: A very large, muscular dog, with a long, tapering head, arched neck and loin, and deep chest. The ears are relatively small, and the tail long. The coat is shaggy, with a bushy beard and eyebrows, and is usually grey, but may be black, white, red or brindle

LURCHER

HEIGHT: 69–76cm (27–30in)
WEIGHT: 27–32kg (60–70lb)
LIFE EXPECTANCY: 12–14 years
ORIGIN: Ireland
DESCRIPTION: Greyhound-like, with a tapering muzzle, deep chest, and arched loin. The ears are small and high-set, the tail long and tapering, often with a curl at the tip. The coat may be short and wiry, long or broken, and occurs in a wide variety of colours

Although the Lurcher is not regarded as a purebred dog, or recognized by most canine societies as it is not bred to a particular standard, it is of a definite and distinctive type, and has been known since at least the 1600s, and probably much earlier. It is thought to have developed as the result of crossbreeding between greyhounds and deerhounds with collies or other herding dogs, and also between these hounds and terriers, such as the Bedlington Terrier, originating at a time when only the nobility were permitted to own purebred sighthounds with which to hunt. The Lurcher has traditionally been used by gypsies for hunting and coursing, and is a very fast and agile dog, which retains a strong hunting instinct and requires a fair amount of exercise. However, it is also gentle, affectionate and intelligent, and can be obedience trained with relative ease.

CANAAN DOG

The Canaan Dog was originally developed in Israel during the 1930s for the security forces, from the semi-wild or feral dogs that had been used by Bedouin tribes-people for hundreds of years as camp and flock guards. Whilst it is still used in these roles, it has also been employed in herding, tracking, mine detection, search and rescue, and as a guide dog for the blind. Highly intelligent, loyal and quick to learn, the breed is now also becoming popular as a family pet, and being naturally protective, it makes a good watchdog and guard dog for the home. However, without socialization when young, the Canaan Dog may be somewhat overprotective, remaining very wary of strangers, being aggressive with other dogs, particularly those of the same sex, and barking excessively. It is also a lively, energetic dog, and requires a fair amount of exercise.

HEIGHT: 48–61cm (19–24in)
WEIGHT: 16–25kg (35–55lb)
LIFE EXPECTANCY: 12–14 years
ORIGIN: Israel
DESCRIPTION: A sturdy, medium-sized dog with a wedge-shaped head, high-set, erect ears, and a bushy tail, which is often carried over the back. The medium-length coat is straight and harsh, and colours include sandy, red, black, white, grey, brindle and white with large patches of colour

IBIZAN HOUND

A very fast and agile sighthound with excellent vision and hearing, the Ibizan Hound was developed on the Spanish island of Ibiza, and other surrounding Balearic islands, where it was employed mainly for hunting rabbits, and in addition to chasing down its quarry, it has been used to both point and retrieve to good effect. This highly elegant breed is very similar in appearance to the Pharaoh Hound, and although it is generally taller, and occurs in a wider variety of colours, both are thought to originate from a common ancestor that was known to the Egyptians several thousand years ago, and which was probably taken to Europe by Phoenician traders. It is still used for hunting to this day, often in packs, but is also favoured for coursing, and as a companion and show dog. This breed makes an excellent pet, but requires a great deal of exercise, and also a secure yard, as it is capable of jumping great heights from a standstill.

HEIGHT: 56–74cm (22–29in)
WEIGHT: 19–25kg (42–55lb)
LIFE EXPECTANCY: 10–12 years
ORIGIN: Spain
DESCRIPTION: An elegant hound, with a long, tapering head, large, highly mobile, triangular ears, and a long, slender tail. The coat occurs in three forms: smooth, long and wire, which may be red, white, red and white or tan and white in colour

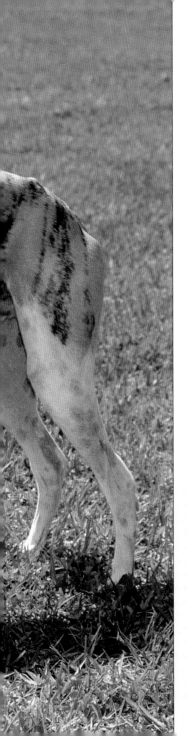

GREYHOUND

Although its exact origins are uncertain, the Greyhound is thought to have descended from ancient Middle Eastern sighthounds such as the Sloughi, and it has been known to man for thousands of years. Its presence in Britain dates at least as far back as 900AD, and since Anglo-Saxon times it has been connected to the English monarchy, used for hunting deer and boar, when such activities were the exclusive preserve of the royal estates. Since that time, it has been used in the coursing of small game, particularly hares, but it is probably best known today as a racing dog, and is thought to be the fastest dog in the world, capable of attaining speeds of over 65km/h (40mph). A popular family companion, the Greyhound has a very gentle and affectionate disposition, and tends to be rather inactive when indoors. However, it requires daily exercise, with the opportunity to run freely, and some individuals may require a muzzle when off the leash due to their instinct for chasing prey.

HEIGHT: 68–76cm (27–30in)
WEIGHT: 27–32kg (60–70lb)
LIFE EXPECTANCY: 10–12 years
ORIGIN: Britain
DESCRIPTION: A highly elegant, muscular dog, with a very deep chest, arched loin, and long, tapering muzzle. The small ears are folded back, and the long tail is carried with a slight curve at the tip. The coat is short and occurs in a wide variety of colours

BASENJI

HEIGHT: 38–43cm (15–17in)
WEIGHT: 9–11kg (20–25lb)
LIFE EXPECTANCY: 10–12 years
ORIGIN: Zaire
DESCRIPTION: A small or medium-sized, smooth-coated dog, with a wrinkled forehead and tightly curled tail. Colours include black, red, copper, black and tan and brindle, usually with white feet, chest and tail-tip

Sometimes known as the Congo Dog, the Basenji originated in Zaire, Africa, where it has been used in packs to hunt game such as antelope, monkeys and small wild cats, probably for thousands of years. Pursuing its quarry by both scent and sight, it drives animals into the open, into nets, or up trees, where they can then be dispatched by its handlers. Quite fearless, the Basenji has even been known to attack large predators such as big cats, particularly in defence of its pups. Interestingly, the Basenji is also known as the African Barkless Dog, and perhaps the most remarkable characteristic of this breed is its unique voice. It is generally silent and does not bark, but produces a variety of yodelling calls. Highly intelligent, affectionate and playful, the Basenji will make a good pet if handled and socialized regularly when young, and is often most content if kept with others of its kind.

PHARAOH HOUND

As its name might suggest, the Pharaoh Hound is thought to have originated from dogs that were known to the ancient Egyptians, and is amongst the oldest of domesticated breeds, but it was actually developed on the Mediterranean island of Malta, probably as the descendant of hounds that were taken there by the Phoenicians. A distinctive, graceful hound with very large ears, the Pharaoh Hound hunts by scent, sight and hearing, and was employed mainly for hunting rabbits, and it is still highly prized by farmers in this role. However, it is also a good watch and guard dog, and has been used to guard sheep and goats, as well as property, and has sometimes also been used as a flushing gundog. The Pharaoh Hound was first introduced to Britain during the 1930s, becoming increasingly popular both there and in the US as a companion breed from the 1960s, but it requires a great deal of exercise if it is to remain content as a pet.

HEIGHT: 53–63cm (21–25in)
WEIGHT: 20–25kg (45–55lb)
LIFE EXPECTANCY: 13–15 years
ORIGIN: Malta
DESCRIPTION: A graceful and athletic sighthound, with a wedge-shaped head and long muzzle. The chest is deep and the loin moderately arched. The tail is tapering and usually carried low, and the ears are large and erect. The coat is short and sleek, and may be red or tan, often with white markings

WHIPPET

The Whippet was developed mainly by working men in the north of England during the latter part of the 19th century as an alternative to the Greyhound, probably by crossbreeding between Greyhounds, Italian Greyhounds and also terriers. The aim was to produce a dog that would occupy less space and be cheaper to feed than a Greyhound, whilst retaining the attributes of speed, agility and stamina, which were necessary for racing, and hare and rabbit coursing. In fact, the Whippet accelerates faster than the Greyhound from a standing start, and may attain speeds of up to 60km/h (37mph). The breed was recognized by the British Kennel Club in 1890, and following the foundation of a breed club some nine years later, it became increasingly popular as a show dog. As a companion, the Whippet tends to be more affectionate than most sighthounds, and is typically docile in the home, but being a sporting breed it will enjoy the opportunity to run freely whenever possible.

HEIGHT: 46–56cm (18–22in)
WEIGHT: 12–14kg (26–31lb)
LIFE EXPECTANCY: 12–14 years
ORIGIN: Britain
DESCRIPTION: A small and slender sighthound, with a tapering muzzle, deep chest, arched neck and loin. The ears are small and rose-shaped, and the tail long, with an upward curve at the tip. The coat is short and sleek and occurs in a wide range of colours and combinations, including brindle, black, red, fawn, white and grey

ITALIAN GREYHOUND

HEIGHT: 30–38cm
(12–15in)
WEIGHT: 3–5kg (6–10lb)
LIFE EXPECTANCY: 13–15
years
ORIGIN: Italy
DESCRIPTION: A small,
elegant greyhound,
with a tapering muzzle,
arched back and loin.
The ears fold back
against the head, the
tail is long, and ends in
a curve. The coat is
short and may be grey,
cream, fawn, black or
blue, often with white
markings on the chest
and feet

The Italian Greyhound is the smallest of the sighthounds, and is an ancient breed, which is thought to have originated around the Mediterranean basin over 2000 years ago, from small hounds that were taken there from the Middle East by the Phoenicians. It is very similar in appearance to the Greyhound, but is much smaller in all its proportions, and from the 16th century onwards, it became a popular companion breed with European royalty and nobility, as witnessed by its inclusion in many 16th and 17th century portrait paintings. An excellent companion, the Italian Greyhound has a lively and affectionate nature, and in practical terms sheds almost no hair, requires little grooming, is virtually odourless and is inexpensive to feed. Despite its somewhat frail appearance, this breed is also hardy and relatively long-lived.

SLOUGHI

Also known as the Arabian Greyhound, the Sloughi is an ancient sighthound whose ancestors are thought to have originated in Africa and parts of the Middle East and representations of similar dogs are commonly found in ancient Egyptian tombs and artefacts. There has been some speculation that the Sloughi may be a form of Saluki or the Azawakh, and like those dogs, it is an incredibly fast and agile breed that was originally employed to hunt gazelle, as well as hares, desert foxes, hyenas and jackals. However, it has also been traditionally employed by the Bedouin as a flock guardian. Although today it is sometimes encountered as both a show dog and pet, the Sloughi remains relatively uncommon, having suffered a serious decline during the 20th century as a result of disrupted breeding programmes, persecution and rabies epidemics. As a pet, the Sloughi is typically devoted and playful, but tends to be somewhat reserved with strangers.

HEIGHT: 61–74cm (24–29in)
WEIGHT: 20–27kg (45–60lb)
LIFE EXPECTANCY: 11–13 years
COUNTRY OF ORIGIN: Morocco
DESCRIPTION: An elegant and athletic sighthound, with a narrow, tapering head, medium-sized, pendant ears and a long, thin tail. The coat is short and soft and occurs in various shades of sand, from pale to red, often with a dark mask and ears

TERRIERS,
PINSCHERS
AND
SCHNAUZERS

AFFENPINSCHER

HEIGHT: 25–38cm (10–15in)
WEIGHT: 3–4kg (7–9lb)
LIFE EXPECTANCY: 10–12 years
ORIGIN: Germany
DESCRIPTION: A small, shaggy terrier, with rounded head and eyes, blunt muzzle and long facial hair. Ears and tail are often docked. Usually black, but variations include grey, silver, brown and black and tan

With its monkey-like face, and playful and inquisitive nature, it is not surprising to learn that in Germany, where this dog originates, its name literally means 'Monkey Terrier', whilst in France, it is known as the 'Diablotin Moustachu' or moustached little devil. It is thought to have first emerged as a distinct breed in the mid 19th century, although its origins are likely to predate this by perhaps 150 to 250 years, and was probably miniaturized from larger working terriers, which were employed to hunt rodents on farms, becoming a domestic pet sometime during the 18th century. To this day, the Affenpinscher remains an effective mouse and rat catcher, and despite its small stature, its alertness and boldness also make it a good watchdog, but today it is most commonly known as a loyal and affectionate companion dog.

GERMAN/STANDARD PINSCHER

The German, or Standard, Pinscher is thought to be descended from old European guardian and herding dogs. In addition to the terriers' traditional role of vermin catcher, this fairly tall breed was employed as a livestock guard, herder and watchdog. Looking rather like a miniature Dobermann, the German Pinscher is known to have played a part in that breed's development, as well as that of the Miniature Pinscher, Affenpinscher and the Schnauzers. By the end of the Second World War it was in danger of dying out, but was restored largely by the efforts of one man, Werner Jung. The German Pinscher makes a loyal and protective companion, which usually responds well to training, but it requires firm handling in order to prevent it from becoming overly dominant and territorial in the home.

HEIGHT: 41–48cm (16–19in)
WEIGHT: 11–16kg (25–35lb)
LIFE EXPECTANCY: 12–14 years
ORIGIN: Germany
DESCRIPTION: A medium-sized, fairly tall terrier, with a long bluntly tipped muzzle, and triangular ears that fold forwards. The ears are often cropped and erect, however, and the tail is typically also docked. The coat is short, smooth and brown or black and tan in colour

MINIATURE PINSCHER

Although the Miniature Pinscher looks somewhat like a small Dobermann, it is a much older breed, and is thought to have been developed from the German or Standard Pinscher, probably with the later addition of Italian Greyhound and Dachshund stock. Like its larger relative, it was originally employed as a ratter, which was used in stables and elsewhere to control vermin, and the word 'pinscher' is derived from its method of pinching, or seizing its quarry. The Miniature Pinscher was first exhibited in Germany in 1900, and rapidly gained in popularity from that time, but it remained largely unknown outside its native country until being introduced to the US around 20 years later, and to Britain in 1938. Being easy to train, playful, alert and fearless, the Miniature Pinscher has since become a popular companion and watchdog. At one time, its ears were often cropped to make them erect, but today it is being bred to have erect ears.

HEIGHT: 25–30cm (10–12in)
WEIGHT: 4–5kg (8–10lb)
LIFE EXPECTANCY: 13–15 years
ORIGIN: Germany
DESCRIPTION: A small, sleek, but muscular dog, with a short, black and tan, red or chocolate coat. The tail is customarily docked short, and the ears may fold forward, but in Europe and the US they are typically cropped and erect

STANDARD SCHNAUZER

HEIGHT: 43–51cm (17–20in)
WEIGHT: 14–20kg (30–45lb)
LIFE EXPECTANCY: 13–15 years
ORIGIN: Germany
DESCRIPTION: A robust, medium-sized dog with a long head, bushy eyebrows, moustache and beard. The ears are triangular and fold forwards, but are sometimes cropped and carried erect, and the tail is typically docked short. The outer coat is harsh and wiry, and may be salt and pepper or black

Thought to be the oldest of the three Schnauzer breeds, the other two being the Giant and the Miniature Schnauzers, the Standard Schnauzer is a medium-sized dog which originated in Germany, where it was probably first employed as a general farm dog, which would have been used for hunting vermin and guarding property, livestock and produce. However, it is a highly versatile breed, which despite possessing something of the tenacious temperament of the terrier, has been successfully trained as a herder, retriever, wartime messenger and also as a performing dog. The Standard Schnauzer has also been popular as a companion breed for hundreds of years, and appears in paintings by such artists as Rembrandt, Dürer, and Joshua Reynolds. It makes a lively, intelligent and affectionate pet, as well as an effective watch and guard dog, but it can be overprotective of both objects and people at times.

MINIATURE SCHNAUZER

Although the Miniature Schnauzer was not recognized as a distinct breed until 1899, Schnauzers have been known in Germany since at least the 1500s, as is evidenced by their inclusion in many artworks during the 16th and 17th century, by such artists as Dürer and Rembrandt. The Schnauzers are closely related to the Pinschers, and the Miniature Schnauzer is thought to have originated from crossbreeding between the Standard Schnauzer and the Affenpinscher, possibly with the later addition of Poodle stock. It was introduced to Britain and the US during the 1920s, and was first employed for controlling vermin in homes and factories, but the Miniature Schnauzer soon became highly regarded as a family companion. Energetic, playful and quick to learn, it has also been used to perform tricks, and its tendency to bark at strangers makes it a good watchdog.

HEIGHT: 30–36cm (12–14in)
WEIGHT: 5–7kg (10–15lb)
LIFE EXPECTANCY: 12–14 years
ORIGIN: Germany
DESCRIPTION: A small, sturdy dog with a long muzzle, with bushy facial hair. The triangular ears fold forward, but may be cropped to stand erect, particularly in the US, and the tail is usually docked. The coat is harsh, and may be black, black and white or black and silver

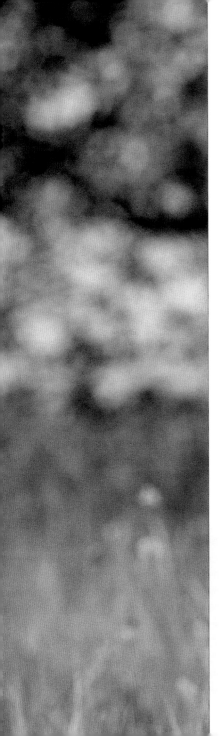

AMERICAN PIT BULL TERRIER

The American Pit Bull Terrier is thought to have originated from Bulldog and terrier crosses, and was first developed as a fighting breed after bull-baiting was outlawed in England in 1835, before being taken to America by settlers during the 19th century, to be used mainly as a working farm dog. It is extremely strong, agile and tenacious, and although it was formerly one of the most popular American breeds, in recent years it has earned a reputation for wilfulness and aggression, and has faced worldwide legislation after a series of reported attacks on people. This reputation is, however, somewhat unjust, for whilst there are those individuals that promote the American Pit Bull's fighting instinct, if properly trained and socialized, this dog is good-natured, companionable and obedient, and excels in every canine role. In fact, an American Pit Bull Terrier named Banddog Dread, holds more working titles than any other dog.

HEIGHT: 46–56cm (18–22in)
WEIGHT: 10–50kg (22–110lb)
LIFE EXPECTANCY: 10–12 years
ORIGIN: USA
DESCRIPTION: A very stocky, muscular dog, with a broad head and neck, and extremely powerful jaws. The ears are often cropped and the tail tapers. The coat is short and shiny, and occurs in many colours and combinations, including black, white, browns, reds, brindle and merle

(ENGLISH)
BULL TERRIER

A very powerful dog, the Bull Terrier was
first developed during the 1800s from
Bulldogs and the Old English Terrier, as a
bull- and badger-baiting breed, and
despite the outlawing of these practices in
England during the 1830s, it continued
to be used illicitly, as well as for dog-
fighting, which was not made illegal until
1911. However, from around the 1850s,
certain breeders began to introduce
pointer and Dalmatian blood, with the
aim of refining both the Bull Terrier's
temperament and appearance, and
establishing the breed as we know it
today. Nicknamed 'The White Cavalier',
the white-coated variety became
popularized by the aristocracy as a
fashionable companion, but the Bull
Terrier continued to be employed in a
variety of other roles, including vermin
control, guarding and even herding. It
remains a popular pet, which thrives on
companionship, but it requires plenty of
exercise, and should be well trained and
socialized when young, as it can
otherwise tend towards aggression with
other dogs.

HEIGHT: 50–60cm (20–24in)
WEIGHT: 20–29kg (45–65lb)
LIFE EXPECTANCY: 10–12 years
ORIGIN: Britain
DESCRIPTION: A stocky, muscular dog, with a
  distinctive, flat-topped head and sloping muzzle.
  Its coat is short and dense, and may be white,
  black, brindle, red, fawn or tri-coloured. The ears
  are held erect, and the tail carried horizontally

STAFFORDSHIRE BULL TERRIER

HEIGHT: 36–41cm (14–16in)
WEIGHT: 11–17kg (25–38lb)
LIFE EXPECTANCY: 12–14 years
ORIGIN: Britain
DESCRIPTION: A compact, muscular dog, with a broad head and powerful jaws. The ears are small and may be rose-like or half-pricked, and the tapering tail is of medium length. The coat is short and sleek, and may be black, blue, fawn or brindle, often with white markings

Named after the English county of Staffordshire where it is thought to have originated, the Staffordshire Bull Terrier was developed as a dog-fighting breed by crossbreeding between Bulldogs and various terriers. However, it was soon to be outclassed as a fighter with the development of the English Bull Terrier, and by 1911, when dog fights were banned in England, its popularity had waned severely. Despite this, the breed survived and through selective breeding its temperament became more biddable, and during the 20th century, the popularity of the Staffordshire Bull Terrier as a companion breed has steadily increased. It remains a fearless and sometimes strong-willed dog, but it is usually also incredibly loyal, affectionate and gentle. In the US, the American Staffordshire Terrier is recognized as a distinct breed, which is typically both taller and heavier. Its ears are often also cropped.

PATTERDALE TERRIER

Developed around the Cumbrian village of Patterdale in the English Lake District, this dog is also known as the Fell, or Black Fell Terrier, and whilst other working terriers, such as the Lakeland Terrier, which originated from the same area, are also sometimes referred to as Patterdale or Fell Terriers, this breed is distinctive on account of its very solid, compact build, broad head, and somewhat Bull Terrier-like expression. In fact, it is thought that the Patterdale Terrier was developed from Bull and Border Terriers, resulting in a very courageous, tenacious dog with a powerful bite, but a generally amiable temperament. It was mainly employed to hunt rodents, rabbits and foxes, particularly in inhospitable conditions over inaccessible terrain where larger dogs could not pursue their quarry, but it is game enough to tackle a badger, and since being introduced to the US in 1978, it has also been used to hunt for marmots and raccoons.

HEIGHT: 25–30cm (10–12in)
WEIGHT: 5–6kg (11–13lb)
LIFE EXPECTANCY: 11–13 years
ORIGIN: Britain
DESCRIPTION: A small, but well-built terrier, with a broad head, small, forward-folding ears, and a fairly short tail. The coat is short and coarse, and may be black, black and tan, red or brown in colour

AIREDALE TERRIER

Originating in the Aire Valley in South Yorkshire, England, the Airedale is the largest of the terriers, and is sometimes referred to as the 'king of terriers' for this reason. The result of crossbreeding between the Otterhound and the Old English Black and Tan Terrier, it is a keen swimmer, and was originally used to hunt otters, polecats, weasels and rats, and until the late 19th century, it was more commonly known as the Waterside Terrier. An intelligent and versatile breed, it was subsequently put to use as a police dog in Britain, France and Russia, and during both the First and Second World Wars, was to prove itself as an effective sentry, messenger and supply carrier. It has also been used to hunt large game, and as a guide dog for the blind, and although some working lines continue, today it is best known as a loyal and hardy companion.

HEIGHT: 56–61cm (22–24in)
WEIGHT: 18–25kg (40–55lb)
LIFE EXPECTANCY: 10–12 years
ORIGIN: Britain
DESCRIPTION: A large, wire-coated terrier, with a long, flattened head and broad chest. Coat is tan overall, with a black back, or saddle, and black top of neck and tail

SOFT-COATED WHEATEN TERRIER

HEIGHT: 43–49cm (17–19in)
WEIGHT: 14–20kg (30 –45lb)
LIFE EXPECTANCY: 12–14
    years
ORIGIN: Ireland
DESCRIPTION: A large, but
    compact terrier, with a
    rectangular head and
    short, strong muzzle. The
    ears are triangular, and
    fold forwards, whilst the
    tail is high-set and
    customarily docked. The
    coat is silky with a slight
    wave, and is black at
    birth, lightening to a
    wheaten colour by about
    two years of age

Although not recognized or shown as a distinct breed in Ireland until the 1930s (in Britain and the US until the 1940s) the Soft-coated Wheaten Terrier is thought to be the oldest of the Irish terriers, and is known to have played a part in the development of the Kerry Blue Terrier. It is a fairly large terrier which was developed as an all-round farm dog and was capable of herding livestock, guarding and controlling vermin, as well as being an adept hunter of small game such as rabbits, badgers and otters. The Soft-coated Wheaten Terrier of today retains its tenacity and remains a keen ratter and rabitter, and whist it can be more difficult to obedience train than some other breeds, it usually makes an affectionate and lively family pet if well trained and thoroughly socialized when young. It also tends to be less aggressive towards other dogs than many terriers.

KERRY BLUE TERRIER

Named after County Kerry in Ireland, where it is thought have been developed during the 18th or 19th century, the Kerry Blue Terrier is considered to be one of the national dogs of Ireland, and is also known there as the Irish Blue Terrier. Its exact origins are uncertain, but it has been suggested that Irish, Welsh, Bedlington, and Soft-coated Wheaten Terriers may have played a part in its development, whilst the Portuguese Water Dog is also often cited as a possible ancestor, contributing to the Kerry Blue Terrier's love of water and distinctive coat. An all-round farm dog, this breed has been employed for hunting rodents and small game, retrieving, herding and guarding, but perhaps more surprisingly, it has also seen use as a police dog. Today, the Kerry Blue Terrier is found mainly as a family companion, and makes an affectionate, if somewhat boisterous pet.

HEIGHT: 46–51cm (18–20in)
WEIGHT: 15–18kg (33–40lb)
LIFE EXPECTANCY: 12–14 years
ORIGIN: Ireland
DESCRIPTION: A medium-sized, muscular terrier, with a soft curly or wavy coat, that occurs in a range of blues, often with darker points. The head is long, with a bushy moustache, beard and eyebrows. The ears are triangular and fold forwards, and the tail is usually docked and carried erect

LAKELAND TERRIER

HEIGHT: 32–38cm (13–15in)

WEIGHT: 7–8kg (15–18lb)

LIFE EXPECTANCY: 12–14 years

ORIGIN: Britain

DESCRIPTION: A medium-sized, wire-coated terrier with an elongated head and bushy facial hair. The ears are small and fold forwards, and the high-set tail is typically docked. The coat may be dark grey, black and tan, reddish, wheaten or liver and blue in colour, often with a dark saddle

The Lakeland Terrier is a medium-sized, wire-coated terrier, which originated in the Lake District in northern England, and although it was once also known as the Patterdale or Fell Terrier, those names have since been assigned to another terrier from the same area, which may be distinguished by its smaller size and shorter, often black coat, which lacks furnishings. However, in such remote locations, the tradition of breeding good working terriers was always of greater importance than adhering to breed standards or even distinguishing between breeds, and the name Patterdale is often applied to a terrier type, as opposed to a distinct breed. The Lakeland Terrier is thought to have been developed from the Old English Wire-haired Terrier and the Bedlington Terrier, and was originally employed to kill mice and rats, as well as larger mammals such as foxes, badgers and otters, but more recently, it has become a popular companion and successful show dog.

WELSH TERRIER

With its long legs and wiry coat, the Welsh Terrier looks much like a miniaturised Airedale, or a slightly stockier Lakeland Terrier, and like the Airedale, it was developed during the 1800s. It was originally employed to kill rats, as well as for hunting a variety of larger animals that were regarded as vermin, including polecats, badgers, otters and foxes. Being able to reach places that were inaccessible to the larger Otter Hound and Foxhound, it would often accompany packs of those dogs as they worked. It was first shown in England in 1884, and by 1886 a breed club had been established, and the Welsh Terrier was recognized by the British Kennel Club. Two years later it was exported to the US, and it has gone on to become a popular show dog and companion breed on both sides of the Atlantic.

HEIGHT: 36–39cm (14–15in)
WEIGHT: 9–10kg (20–22lb)
LIFE EXPECTANCY: 10–12 years
ORIGIN: Britain
DESCRIPTION: A compact but fairly long-legged terrier, with a long, rectangular head, bushy eyebrows, moustache and beard. The ears are triangular and fold forwards and the high-set tail is typically docked. The coat is wiry, and is black, or black grizzle, and tan

WIRE FOX TERRIER & SMOOTH FOX TERRIER

Formerly regarded as varieties of the same dog, the Wire Fox Terrier and Smooth Fox Terrier have in recent years become more commonly recognized as distinct breeds, although with the exception of their coats, they are essentially identical. Both were developed for foxhunting alongside hounds, employed to locate and flush a fox if it went to ground, and have also proved themselves adept at rat catching and hunting other small animals. However, they are thought to have been developed independently, with the wire-coated form used to work over rougher terrain. Some sources suggest that the Wire Fox Terrier may have been developed by breeding the smooth-coated dog with older forms of wire-haired terrier, whilst others record the Smooth Fox Terrier as a later breed. Energetic, inquisitive and playful, Fox Terriers are mainly found as companion dogs today, but they can be boisterous and aggressive, particularly with other dogs, cats and wild animals. They may also bark excessively.

HEIGHT: 33–41cm (13–16in)
WEIGHT: 6–9kg (13–20lb)
LIFE EXPECTANCY: 13–15 years
ORIGIN: Britain
DESCRIPTION: Fairly tall and short-backed, with a slender, tapering head, small ears that fold forwards, and a high-set tail, which is normally docked. The coat is usually predominantly white, with black, tan, or black and tan markings, and may be smooth or wiry, according to breed

BEDLINGTON TERRIER

HEIGHT: 38–43cm (15–17in)
WEIGHT: 8–10kg (18–22lb)
LIFE EXPECTANCY: 12–16
  years
ORIGIN: Britain
DESCRIPTION: A lean, long-
  legged terrier, with an
  arched back and, narrow,
  sloping head. Its coat is
  dense, with a woolly
  appearance, contributing
  to this breed's overall
  sheep-like look. Colours
  include blue, black and
  tan, sandy and liver

A hardy and usually long-lived breed, the Bedlington
Terrier's lamb-like appearance belies its fearlessness,
tenacity and stamina. Sometimes also known as the
Rothbury Terrier, it was developed around the area of
Rothbury on the Scottish and English borders during
the 1800s, to catch wild animals such as rats, rabbits,
hares, foxes, otters and badgers, but was also used as
a fighting dog. Its exact origins are somewhat
uncertain, but the Dandie Dinmont Terrier, the
Whippet and various wire-coated terriers are
believed to have contributed to its development, and
today it is often crossed with Greyhounds and
Whippets in order to produce lurchers. An
affectionate and loyal family pet, the Bedlington
Terrier requires socialization when young in order to
reduce its aggressive tendencies towards other dogs.

IRISH TERRIER

Although it was not standardized until the emergence of breed clubs during the 19th century, the Irish Terrier, or Irish Red Terrier, is thought to be amongst the oldest of terrier breeds. It originates from County Cork in Ireland, where it has been used as a watchdog, guard dog and hunter of vermin for hundreds of years. It has also been used by police and military forces, and despite its relatively small size, this dog is highly tenacious and exceptionally brave. The Irish Terrier is a loyal, affectionate and protective companion, which will guard its home and family with no thought for its own safety. However, it can be somewhat wilful, and is often aggressive towards other dogs, and should therefore be well trained and thoroughly socialized when young. It is also a very active, inquisitive and lively dog, which requires a fair amount of both physical and mental stimulation in order to remain content.

HEIGHT: 46–48cm (18–19in)
WEIGHT: 11–12kg (25–27lb)
LIFE EXPECTANCY: 12–14 years
ORIGIN: Ireland
DESCRIPTION: A fairly tall terrier, with a long head, bearded muzzle, bushy eyebrows and moustache. The ears are small, triangular and fold forwards, whilst the tail is often docked and carried erect. The coat is short and wiry, and may be red, golden or wheaten in colour

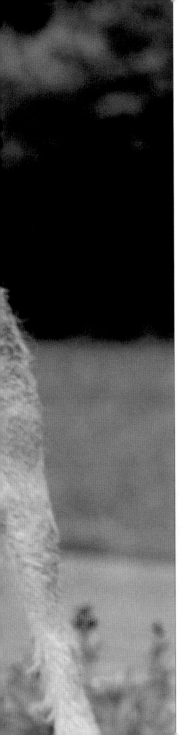

BORDER TERRIER

Probably developed from dogs such as the Dandie Dinmont and other terriers, the Border Terrier originated in the Cheviot Hills area, in the Border counties of England and Scotland, where it was used primarily to hunt mice, rats, and, despite its small size, also foxes, martens and otters. With its relatively long legs and abundant stamina, this dog was able to hunt alongside horses, and on account of its tenacity was capable of tackling badgers, whilst its wiry coat protected it from the frequently inclement weather of the region. As with many of the terrier breeds that were initially found only as working farm dogs, the Border Terrier gradually became more popular in the home, and although today it is a common family pet and a show dog, it is still used on farms to control vermin. Affectionate, easy to train and economical to feed, the Border Terrier makes a good companion, but it is very lively and requires a lot of exercise for such a small dog.

HEIGHT: 28–31cm (11–12in)
WEIGHT: 5–7kg (11–15lb)
LIFE EXPECTANCY: 12–16 years
ORIGIN: Britain
DESCRIPTION: A small terrier with a short muzzle, small ears, and a fairly short, tapering tail, which is often carried level to its back. The coat is coarse and wiry, and may be red, tan, blue and tan or grizzle and tan, sometimes with small patches of white on the chest

GLEN OF IMAAL TERRIER

HEIGHT: 33–36cm
(13–14in)
WEIGHT: 14–16kg
(32–35lb)
LIFE EXPECTANCY: 12–14
years
ORIGIN: Ireland
DESCRIPTION: A medium-
sized, short-legged and
long-bodied terrier,
with small ears and a
short tail, which is
usually docked to half
its length. The coat is
harsh and shaggy, and
may be red, blue,
brindle or wheaten in
colour

Although various forms of terrier had been recognized far
earlier, little distinction was made between them until
about the 19th century, when selective breeding began to
result in more clearly defined types. However, the Glen of
Imaal appears relatively unrefined to this day, bearing
features that were at one time shared by several early
terriers, such as its slightly out-turned feet, and rose-like,
or half-pricked ears. It is named after the Glen of Imaal, in
County Wicklow, Ireland, where it is thought to have
originated as a hardy vermin hunter, which was used to
hunt rats, foxes and badgers. A tenacious and silent hunter,
the Glen of Imaal Terrier continues to be employed as a
ratter, but today it is more commonly encountered as a
family companion. This breed makes an affectionate, loyal
and lively pet, but as with many terriers, it can be
somewhat stubborn, and aggressive to other dogs at times.

MANCHESTER TERRIER

Probably developed from the Whippet, and the Black and Tan Terrier of old, the Manchester Terrier is still sometimes known as the Black and Tan Terrier, but it is also sometimes colloquially referred to as the 'rat terrier', due to its abilities as a vermin hunter. However, that name is now more commonly used to describe a distinct breed, which was developed in the US by crossbreeding the Manchester Terrier with other breeds, including the Beagle. Intelligent, tenacious and agile, in addition to ratting, the Manchester Terrier was used to hunt rabbits, but today it is most commonly found as a family pet. This breed is generally affectionate, playful and responsive, but can be wilful and wary with strangers, and should therefore be well socialized when young. A smaller form, the English Toy Terrier, also occurs.

HEIGHT: 38–41cm (15–16in)
WEIGHT: 5–10kg (12–22lb)
LIFE EXPECTANCY: 13–15 years
ORIGIN: Britain
DESCRIPTION: A small, elegant terrier, with an arched back and loin, and a long, tapering muzzle. The ears are small and fold forwards, and the tail is thin and tapering. The coat is short and sleek, and black with rich tan markings

(PARSON) JACK RUSSELL TERRIER

Often known simply as the Jack Russell, this compact terrier takes its name from the 19th century English clergyman who developed the breed, and it is also sometimes known as the Parson Jack Russell. Various terrier breeds are thought to have contributed to its development, and there remains a great deal of variation in the size, shape and weight of today's dogs, with short- and long-legged, as well as smooth, broken and rough-coated individuals occurring. Long-legged, rough-coated dogs are often similar in appearance to the Wire Fox Terrier, and in addition to hunting for vermin such as mice and rats, the Jack Russell was also employed to hunt larger animals such as foxes, which it would flush or dig from the ground. Brave and tenacious in the field, this spirited dog is generally also active and playful indoors, and it can be somewhat wilful if not well trained when young. It should also be extensively socialized, as it often has a tendency towards aggression with other dogs.

HEIGHT: 25–38cm (10–15in)
WEIGHT: 6–8kg (14–18lb)
LIFE EXPECTANCY: 13–15 years
ORIGIN: Britain
DESCRIPTION: A small, compact dog, with a muscular neck and fairly narrow chest. The ears are triangular and fold forwards, and the high-set tail is often docked. The coat is mainly white, with black, red, tan or brown markings, and occurs in smooth, broken and wire-haired forms

AUSTRALIAN TERRIER

HEIGHT: 23–28cm (9–11in)
WEIGHT: 4–6kg (9–13lb)
LIFE EXPECTANCY: 12–15 years
ORIGIN: Australia
DESCRIPTION: A small, short-legged terrier with a fairly long body, and small, erect ears. The coat is rough, of medium length overall, but shorter on the lower legs, and with a ruff around the neck. Colours include blue and tan, sandy or red. The tail is typically docked

One of only a few terriers developed outside the British Isles, the Australian Terrier's origins can, however, be traced back to Britain. It is amongst the smallest of the working terriers, but displays the self-assuredness of a much larger dog, being tenacious, fearless and hardy, and it was originally used to destroy rats and snakes, as a watchdog, and even to herd sheep. It has also always been a loyal companion dog, and makes a good family pet, although it needs to be kept active, on account of its high energy and intelligence levels. This breed will also usually require close supervision when being walked, as it will habitually chase small animals such as rabbits, squirrels and cats, but it is generally considered easier to train than other terriers, and can do well in obedience trials.

NORFOLK TERRIER

This small, hardy dog is amongst the most recently recognized of terriers, only being accepted as a distinct breed in 1964. Until that time it had been regarded as a drop-eared variety of the Norwich Terrier. Like the Norwich Terrier, the Norfolk Terrier was first employed as a farm dog, which was used to control rat and rabbit populations in and around farm buildings and fields, but it will readily go to ground, is small and game enough to flush a fox from its den, and has been used in packs by foxhunters, with the result that this breed is often more sociable with other dogs than is typical for a terrier. Active and affectionate, the Norfolk Terrier makes a good family pet, which enjoys the outdoor life.

HEIGHT: 23–25cm (9–10in)
WEIGHT: 5–6kg (11–13lb)
LIFE EXPECTANCY: 12–14 years
ORIGIN: Britain
DESCRIPTION: A small, compact and angular terrier, with small, forward-folding ears. The tail is usually docked short, and the coat is wiry, and may be red, wheaten, black and tan, or grizzle, sometimes with white markings

CAIRN TERRIER

Originally known as the Short-haired Skye Terrier, the Cairn Terrier originates from the Isle of Skye, off the coast of northwest Scotland. It is thought to be amongst the oldest of terriers, and as such, it is most likely the ancestor of other Scottish terrier breeds, such as the Skye Terrier and West Highland White Terrier. Its name is derived from the cairns, or piles of stones that have been used on the island as markers since ancient times, amongst which this terrier was probably employed to rout out animals such as rats, foxes, badgers and other small mammals that would have been regarded as vermin. Now mainly a companion dog, this inquisitive, highly active breed is nevertheless affectionate and relatively easy to train, and it may excel at such activities as competitive obedience and performing tricks.

HEIGHT: 23–33cm (9–13in)
WEIGHT: 6–8kg (13–18lb)
LIFE EXPECTANCY: 12–14 years
ORIGIN: Britain
DESCRIPTION: A small, shaggy terrier, with a broad head and relatively short muzzle. The ears are small and erect, and the tail short. The coat is of medium length, and may be cream, grey, red, almost black or brindle in colour

NORWICH TERRIER

HEIGHT: 23–25cm (9–10in)
WEIGHT: 5–6kg (11–13lb)
LIFE EXPECTANCY: 12–14 years
ORIGIN: Britain
DESCRIPTION: A small, sturdy terrier, with a rounded body and fox-like muzzle. The ears are erect and the tail typically docked short. The coat is wiry and may be red, wheaten, black and tan, or grizzle, sometimes with white markings

The Norwich Terrier is amongst the smallest of working terriers, and is thought to have been developed from old Black and Tan Terriers, probably with the later introduction of Staffordshire Bull, Bedlington and Irish Terrier stock. The Norwich Terrier is most easily distinguished from the Norfolk Terrier by its erect, rather than forward-folding ears, but it is also somewhat more rounded and less angular. Originating as a farm dog, the Norwich Terrier was used to hunt for vermin and also rabbits, but as with most terriers it is tenacious, powerful for a dog of its size, with a strong bite, and it was also used to dig out and flush foxes if they went to ground during a hunt. Although still highly regarded as a ratter, today the Norwich Terrier is found mainly as a companion dog, and makes an affectionate, playful pet.

DANDIE DINMONT TERRIER

Although various terrier types were recognized much earlier, up until about the early 19th century, little distinction was made in terms of breeds, and in 1815, the Dandie Dinmont Terrier was amongst the first to be named. Its name is derived from the fictional character and terrier owner, Dandie Dinmont, who featured in the popular Sir Walter Scott novel *Guy Mannering*. The Dandie Dinmont was used for controlling rodent populations, as well as for catching rabbits, otters, foxes, polecats and badgers, and although today it is most commonly found as a family companion, it retains a strong hunting instinct. Therefore, whilst this breed is affectionate, intelligent and lively, it can at times also be independent, stubborn and wilful.

HEIGHT: 20–28cm (8–11in)
WEIGHT: 8–11kg (18–24lb)
LIFE EXPECTANCY: 12–14 years
ORIGIN: Britain
DESCRIPTION: A small terrier, with short legs, pendant ears, and a tail that is carried in an upward curve. The coat is distinctive, being soft on the underparts and harsher above, with a silky topknot on the head. It may be mustard (tan) or pepper (grey) in colour

WEST HIGHLAND WHITE TERRIER

Whilst it has sometimes been suggested that the West Highland White Terrier, or Westie, as it is affectionately known, is merely a white form of the Cairn Terrier, it is without doubt a distinct breed. However, as with many Scottish Terriers, it is likely that the Cairn Terrier has played some part in its evolution. The breed as we know it today was developed principally by a Colonel E. D. Malcolm in Poltalloch in Argyllshire, Scotland, during the 1800s, and for a time was known as the Poltalloch Terrier. Hardy and tenacious, this breed was originally employed to hunt foxes and other vermin in the rocky Highlands, and although it has lost none of its gameness or agility, it is a playful and affectionate dog, which thrives on human companionship and is also relatively easy to train. Since it was first exhibited in 1907, the West Highland White Terrier has gone on to become a popular pet and a highly successful show dog.

HEIGHT: 23–30cm (9–12in)
WEIGHT: 7–10kg (15–22lb)
LIFE EXPECTANCY: 13–15 years
ORIGIN: Britain
DESCRIPTION: A small, compact terrier, with a dense, shaggy white coat, and somewhat fox-like face. The ears are small, pointed and erect, and the medium-length tail is carried jauntily

SCOTTISH TERRIER

Popularly known as the 'Scottie', this familiar little terrier is distinctive on account of its short legs, elongated head and bushy facial hair. It is thought to have originated in the Highlands and Western Islands of Scotland, and to have been developed in an earlier form during the 1700s, but it has only been known in its present form since the late 19th century, when it was first exhibited. It was initially referred to as the Aberdeen Terrier, but became officially known as the Scottish Terrier when it was registered with the British Kennel Club in 1897. A strong, hardy, active and low-set dog, the Scottish Terrier was employed as a ratter, and also for hunting larger animals in their burrows, including rabbits, foxes, otters and badgers. Today it is a popular companion breed in many countries around the world, and is also very successful as a show dog.

HEIGHT: 25–28 cm (10–11in)
WEIGHT: 8–10kg (18–22lb)
LIFE EXPECTANCY: 12–14 years
ORIGIN: Britain
DESCRIPTION: A compact, short-legged terrier, with an elongated muzzle and bushy facial hair. The ears are pointed and carried erect, and the tail is of medium length. The coat is coarse, and may be black, grey, wheaten or brindle

RAT TERRIER

HEIGHT: 25–48cm (10–19in)
WEIGHT: 3–16kg (6–35lb)
LIFE EXPECTANCY: 14–16 years
ORIGIN: USA
DESCRIPTION: A compact but muscular dog, with a deep chest, small head and pointed muzzle. The ears are relatively large, and usually held erect, whilst tails may be long or short, and are sometimes docked. Coat colours include red, red and white, and black and tan

Occurring in a range of sizes, Rat Terrier-types were produced in Britain by crossbreeding between Manchester Terriers and Smooth Fox Terriers, but it was in the US that the breed was developed, with the further addition of Fox Terrier blood, as well as Whippet, Italian Greyhound and Beagle stock. The result was a dog that combined both terrier and hound-like qualities, with a strong hunting urge and excellent ratting ability, but a biddable temperament. Some smaller individuals are thought to have arisen by crossbreeding between the Smooth Fox Terrier, Chihuahua and other breeds. An excellent farm dog, watchdog and companion, the Rat Terrier is lively and affectionate, but can be somewhat stubborn when young. The breed is thought to have been named by Theodore Roosevelt who owned three of these dogs.

(AUSTRALIAN) SILKY TERRIER

Looking much like the Yorkshire Terrier, it is thought that the Silky Terrier originated during the 19th century by crossbreeding between the Australian Terrier and the Yorkshire Terrier, with further strains of the Dandie Dinmont and Skye Terrier being added with the aim of improving the quality of its coat. However, most standards require the Silky Terrier to be blue and tan rather than steel-grey and tan, and that the coat should not reach the ground, as in the Yorkshire Terrier. The breed was first established in Sydney, and was not widely known outside Australia until the Second World War, when servicemen stationed there began to introduce it to the US. Today this toy breed has become a popular companion and show dog around the world, but it retains the tenacity of other terriers, and is a capable vermin hunter.

HEIGHT: 23–25cm (9–10in)
WEIGHT: 4–5kg (8–11lb)
LIFE EXPECTANCY: 12–14 years
ORIGIN: Australia
DESCRIPTION: A compact, lightly built, long haired terrier, with erect triangular ears, and a high-set tail, which is customarily docked short. The coat is fine and silky, and is blue and tan in colour

YORKSHIRE TERRIER

Despite its dainty appearance, which is perhaps accentuated by the common practice of tying up its topknot in a ribbon, the Yorkshire Terrier was first employed as a ratter and hunter of other vermin, and was initially larger than is typical today. It is thought to have been developed from such terriers as the now extinct Clydesdale, the Skye, the old Black and Tan, and also the Maltese, and it has gradually been miniaturized by a process of selective breeding in order to produce the small companion and highly successful show dog known today. It was originally known as the Broken-haired Scottish Terrier, but much of its development occurred in the English County of Yorkshire, and when it was officially recognized by the British Kennel Club in 1889, it became known as the Yorkshire Terrier. Although it is generally an affectionate pet, it retains the tenacity imbued by its heritage, and may be aggressive towards other dogs, strangers and small animals.

HEIGHT: 15–23cm (6–9in)
WEIGHT: 2–3kg (4–7lb)
LIFE EXPECTANCY: 12–14 years
ORIGIN: Britain
DESCRIPTION: A small, but sturdy terrier, with a distinctive steel-blue and tan coat, comprised of long, silky hair, which parts along the back, and may reach the ground. The ears are small and carried erect, as is the tail, which usually docked

TOY AND COMPANION BREEDS

KEESHOND

Thought to be closely related to the Samoyed and Elkhound, this medium-sized, spitz-type dog originated in the Netherlands, and is the national dog of Holland. It takes its name from the 18th century Dutch political leader Cornelius de Gyzeluar, who was known as Kees, and who chose the dog as his mascot. However, the Keeshond is also sometimes known as the Wolf Spitz, on account of its wolf-grey coat, and at one time it was popularly referred to as the Dutch Barge Dog, as it was used as a ratter, watchdog and guard dog on the canal boats that travelled between Holland and Germany. Intelligent, affectionate and alert, the Keeshond makes an excellent companion, which is usually amiable with both people and other dogs, but like other spitz breeds, it also has an independent nature, can be wilful at times, and may be predisposed to bark at strangers.

HEIGHT: 44–48cm (17–19in)
WEIGHT: 20–30kg (45–66lb)
LIFE EXPECTANCY: 12–14 years
ORIGIN: Holland
DESCRIPTION: A medium-sized spitz-type dog, with a profuse, grey coat, erect triangular ears, and a medium-length tail which is carried tightly curled on its back

POMERANIAN

HEIGHT: 20–28cm (8–11in)
WEIGHT: 2–3kg (4–7lb)
LIFE EXPECTANCY: 14–16 years
ORIGIN: Germany
DESCRIPTION: A very small, spitz-type dog, with a wedge-shaped head, pointed erect ears, and a feathered tail, which is often carried over the back. The coat is profuse, with an abundant ruff around the neck and chest, and may be red, cream, blue, brown or black in colour, and is sometimes parti-coloured

The Pomeranian originated in an area of northern Germany known as Pomerania during the 1800s, and is the smallest member of the spitz group of dogs. It is probably descended from the larger Standard, or Mittel, German Spitz, which was used as a general farm dog and herding breed, but the Pomeranian was essentially bred as a lapdog and was deliberately reduced in size through a process of selective breeding. It was popularized in Britain during the late 19th century, partly by Queen Victoria, who is known to have kept this dog, and who later established breeding kennels and successfully exhibited the Pomeranian at Crufts Dog Show. This breed is intelligent and quick to learn, which has seen it become popular as both a performing dog and companion, whilst its tendency to bark at strangers makes it a good watchdog. However, this behaviour can often be reduced with training if desired.

BICHON FRISÉ

Also known as the Tenerife Dog, this breed is thought to have originated on the Mediterranean island of Tenerife in the 14th century, as the result of crossbreeding between the Poodle and the Barbet Water Spaniel, and transported to other parts of Europe by sailors, who frequently offered the dog as trade. It became highly popular in both France and Spain, where it was a favourite of the royal courts during the 16th century, as evidenced by its frequent inclusion in royal portraiture around that time. However, by the 1700s, the Bichon Frisé was more commonly found as the organ grinders' companion of choice, or performing in the circus. Bold and intelligent with an amenable temperament, today it is a popular pet and show

HEIGHT: 23–30cm (9–12in)
WEIGHT: 3–5kg (7–12lb)
LIFE EXPECTANCY: 14–16 years
ORIGIN: Mediterranean
DESCRIPTION: Small and compact, with a 'powder-puff' coat, and plume-like tail, which is carried over the back. Small black eyes and nose contrast starkly with the coat, which may be all white, or show traces of cream, apricot or grey

BOLOGNESE

HEIGHT: 25–30cm (10–12in)
WEIGHT: 3–4kg (7–9lb)
LIFE EXPECTANCY: 12–14 years
ORIGIN: Italy
DESCRIPTION: Small bichon dog, compact, and covered with a pure white, fluffy coat, which is long overall, but shorter on the muzzle. The tail is typically carried over the back

A member of the bichon group of dogs, the Bolognese, or Bichon Bolognese, as it is sometimes also known, is thought to have descended from bichon-type dogs in southern Italy, around the 11th or 12th century. Like the Bichon Frisé, it became popular as a companion dog amongst the royal courts and nobility of Spain, and other parts of Europe from the 1500s to the early 19th century, and bichons are featured in several paintings by artists such as Titian and Goya. Generally somewhat less active than the Bichon Frisé, the Bolognese is nevertheless a playful and friendly breed, which will form a close bond with its owner. It is also intelligent, easy to train, and eager to please, making it an ideal companion dog and family pet, although it may initially be somewhat reserved with strangers.

COTON DE TULEAR

This breed's name is derived from a combination of the French word for cotton, on account of its fluffy, white coat, and the port city of Tulear in Madagascar, where it is thought to have originated around the 15th century, as the descendant of bichon-type dogs carried on French ships and possibly local terriers. It is thought to have remained on the island in isolation for many years, being introduced to the wider world relatively recently. As such, it remains comparatively unknown to this day, although its popularity in Europe and the US is currently increasing. An intelligent and playful dog, the Coton de Tulear will often jump and walk on its hind legs, and it is also a healthy and long-lived breed, that shows no signs of the genetically inherited defects or conditions from which many pedigree breeds so unfortunately suffer.

HEIGHT: 25–30cm (10–12in)
WEIGHT: 5–7kg (12–15lb)
LIFE EXPECTANCY: 14–16 years
ORIGIN: Madagascar
DESCRIPTION: A small, bichon-type dog, with a coat of long fluffy hair. The coat is usually white in colour, sometimes yellowish around the ears and muzzle, but it also occurs in black and white

MALTESE

A small, white, long-haired, bichon-type, the Maltese is a very ancient dog, which is thought to be amongst the oldest of European breeds, and there is evidence of its existence in the Mediterranean area which dates at least as far back as the first century AD. It was probably introduced to Malta by the Phoenicians, later being favoured by the ancient Greeks and Romans, and it may have been first introduced to Britain by returning crusaders. Thought to have been first employed for catching rats, the Maltese became highly popular as a companion to European royalty and nobility, and for many hundreds of years it was particularly popular with women of the royal courts, as an accessory, plaything and bed-warmer. The Maltese remains popular as a lapdog, and since first being exhibited in England in 1864, it has been well-regarded as a show dog. However, it is somewhat terrier-like, and can be tenacious and strong willed.

HEIGHT: 21–25cm (8–10in)
WEIGHT: 2–3kg (4–7lb)
LIFE EXPECTANCY: 14–16 years
ORIGIN: Malta
DESCRIPTION: A small, bichon-type dog, with a luxurious, silky, straight, white coat, which is parted along the back and reaches to the ground in adults. The ears are quite long and pendant, and the plumed tail is carried curled over the back

LÖWCHEN

HEIGHT: 25–33cm (10–13in)
WEIGHT: 4–8kg (9–18lb)
LIFE EXPECTANCY: 12–14 years
ORIGIN: France
DESCRIPTION: A small, bichon-type dog, with a short, broad head, pendant, feathered ears and a medium-length tail, which is carried curled over the back. The coat is long and wavy, often distinctively cut, and colours include white, black, lemon, tan and grey

A small, bichon-type dog, the Löwchen is also known as the 'Little Lion Dog', due to the fact that it is traditionally given a distinctive 'lion-cut', that is, its coat is trimmed in such a way as to resemble that of a lion. The breed originated in France during the 1500s, and is known to have been styled in this way for hundreds of years. Like other bichons, the Löwchen became a highly popular companion dog in royal courts throughout much of Europe, and it is featured in several paintings by the Old Masters. However, by the 20th century this breed's popularity had waned severely, to the extent that during the 1960s, it was recorded as the world's rarest breed. More recently, interest in this lively, affectionate dog has been renewed, but it remains somewhat uncommon.

TOY POODLE

The Toy Poodle is the smallest of the three Poodle varieties, but is in every other respect identical to the larger, Miniature and Standard forms, and is judged by the same standards at competitive dog shows. However, initially the process of miniaturization, which was accomplished by breeding from the smallest, and often weakest, offspring from the litters of Miniature Poodles, resulted in dogs that were considered almost deformed, and which encountered a variety of health problems in later life. Despite these setbacks, due to the concerted efforts of serious breeders, such problems were gradually overcome, resulting in a dog which exhibits all the attractiveness, hardiness and general good nature of its larger relatives, and although its size renders it essentially as a toy breed, it is sometimes grouped as a utility dog along with them, reflecting its working ancestry.

HEIGHT: 25–28cm (10–11in)
WEIGHT: 3–6kg (6–13lb)
LIFE EXPECTANCY: 12–14 years
ORIGIN: France
DESCRIPTION: A small dog, with a long, straight muzzle, broad, pendant ears, and a high-set tail, which is typically docked by half. The coat is dense and curly, and is often clipped short overall, or given a continental, or saddle clip, leaving 'pom-poms' on the ankles, thighs and tail-tip. It occurs in a wide range of solid colours

MINIATURE POODLE

Whilst the Miniature Poodle was developed from the Standard Poodle, it is thought that that breed is probably now somewhat larger than it once was, and that the Miniature form may in fact be closer in size to the original dog. And although the Standard Poodle was originally employed as a gundog, the refined Miniature Poodle of today almost certainly lacks the strength to be effective in such a role. It remains a sporty and highly trainable dog, however, which has seen it become one of the most popular of performing dogs, particularly in its native France, where it has long been a favourite in the circus ring. The Miniature Poodle also became incredibly popular as a companion breed following the Second World War, and by the 1960s it was probably one of the most commonly owned of all dogs. An intelligent and sensitive pet, the Miniature Poodle also makes an excellent watchdog, and for a relatively small breed can put on an impressive display of fierceness.

HEIGHT: 28–38cm (11–15in)
WEIGHT: 7–8kg (15–17lb)
LIFE EXPECTANCY: 12–14 years
ORIGIN: France
DESCRIPTION: A small to medium-sized dog, with a long, straight muzzle, broad, pendant ears, and a high-set tail, which is typically docked by half. The coat is profuse, wiry and curly, and is often clipped short overall, or given a continental, or saddle clip, leaving 'pom-poms' on the ankles, thighs and tail-tip. It occurs in a wide range of solid colours

BRUSSELS GRIFFON/GRIFFON BRUXELLOIS

HEIGHT: 18–20cm (7–8in)
WEIGHT: 4–5kg (8–10lb)
LIFE EXPECTANCY: 12–14 years
ORIGIN: Belgium
DESCRIPTION: A small, compact dog, with a Pug-like face, and a high-set tail, which is often docked. The small ears are also set high, and are often cropped. Coat may be short and smooth, or wiry, and occurs in red, black, reddish-brown and black, and black and tan

In Britain and the US, the Brussels Griffon is usually regarded as a single breed, which is recognized in two varieties: the rough-coated Griffon Bruxellois, and the smooth-coated Petit Brabançon. However, in much of Europe, a further distinction is made between rough-coated individuals on the grounds of colour, with only red dogs being known as the Griffon Bruxellois, or Brussels Griffon, whilst those of other colours, such as black, are known as the Griffon Belge, or Belgian Griffon. Whilst the exact origins of these dogs is somewhat uncertain, it is thought that Belgian stable dogs, which were used to catch rats and other vermin, were crossed with the Affenpinscher, Pug and King Charles Spaniel, in order to produce the varieties known today. Today, it is a popular companion dog.

CHINESE CRESTED DOG

Although there is evidence, both written and archaeological, that suggests this breed has been known to the Chinese for thousands of years, debate continues as to whether these dogs originated in China, other parts of Asia, Africa or even the Americas. Regardless of its exact origins, it was first shown in the West in 1885, and was popularized in the US during the late 19th and early 20th centuries, mainly by three women: Ida Garrett, Debra Woods and Jo Ann Orlik, up until the foundation of the American Chinese Crested Club in 1979. Worldwide promotion of the breed was then taken up by the American entertainer Gypsy Rose Lee, and most Chinese Crested Dogs today can trace their ancestry to lines established by her and Debra Woods. Two distinct forms exist, the Hairless, which has hair on its head, feet and tail, and the Powder Puff, which has a long, silky coat.

HEIGHT: 28–33cm (11–13in)
WEIGHT: 3–6kg (7–13lb)
LIFE EXPECTANCY: 10–12 years
ORIGIN: China and Africa
DESCRIPTION: A small, slender dog, with a rounded head, large erect ears and fairly long muzzle. There are two varieties; one is hairless except for its crested head, feet and tail, the other has a long silky coat. Both are found in various colours, and the skin of the Hairless is often spotted

AMERICAN HAIRLESS TERRIER

HEIGHT: 20–46cm (8–18in)
WEIGHT: 3–8kg (6–18lb)
LIFE EXPECTANCY: 14–16 years
ORIGIN: USA
DESCRIPTION: A medium-sized, muscular terrier with erect 'bat ears'. Hairless except for eyebrows and whiskers, the skin is pinkish, with variously sized, black, brown, red or grey spots

In 1972, a completely hairless female pup was born amongst a litter of Rat Terriers, which would go on to produce a further three hairless pups in her lifetime. It was from these dogs that the American Hairless Terrier was developed, and established as a breed in its own right. Usually born with a sparse, fuzzy coat, this is shed within about six weeks, and as an adult, the American Hairless Terrier remains totally hairless except for its eyebrows and whiskers. Unlike some other hairless breeds, this dog typically exhibits no genetic abnormalities or health problems, and makes for an affectionate, intelligent and lively pet. However, it may be territorial and feisty, particularly with strangers, and in hot weather, requires protection from the sun.

MEXICAN HAIRLESS DOG

Also known as the Xoloitzcuintle or Tepeizeuintli, the Mexican Hairless Dog occurs in three forms: Miniature, Toy and Standard, which are identical in all but size. Approximately a third of each size are also Powder Puff individuals, which possess a fine, downy coat, and although these cannot be exhibited at shows, they are regarded as important in maintaining the breed. The exact origins of the Mexican Hairless are uncertain, but it is an ancient dog that was known to the Aztecs, who kept it as a companion, used it for ritual sacrifice, and also ate its flesh. It became a popular pet in the US during the 19th century, but by the 1950s its numbers had declined severely. Renewed interest in this affectionate, loyal and intelligent dog has spared it from extinction, but even today, the Mexican Hairless remains uncommon.

HEIGHT: 28–56cm (11–22in)
WEIGHT: 4–14kg (9–31lb)
LIFE EXPECTANCY: 13–15 years
ORIGIN: Mexico
DESCRIPTION: A small to medium-sized dog, with an elegant build, and long, tapering tail, with a tuft of hair at the tip. The bare skin may be black, reddish, grey or bronzy, sometimes with pink or brown spots, but coated individuals also occur

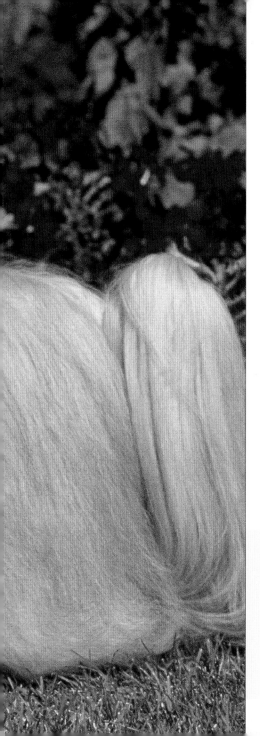

LHASA APSO

Thought to be closely related to the larger Tibetan Terrier, the Lhasa Apso is sometimes known as the Tibetan Apso, and it is an ancient breed, which, as its name would suggest, is native to Tibet. There, it was referred to as a 'lion dog', and used as a watchdog in monasteries and temples, where it was regarded as a sacred protector of Buddha, and also believed to act as a receptacle for its master's soul at the time of their death. For perhaps thousands of years it remained largely unknown outside Tibet, but as this dog was believed to bestow good fortune upon its owner, the Dalai Lama occasionally presented it to visiting foreign dignitaries, bringing the breed to the attention of the wider world. It was first introduced to Britain during the 1920s and to North America in the 1930s, since which time this friendly and responsive dog has become increasingly popular as a pet.

HEIGHT: 25–28cm (10–11in)
WEIGHT: 6–7kg (13–15lb)
LIFE EXPECTANCY: 15–16 years
ORIGIN: Tibet
DESCRIPTION: A small but sturdy dog, with a medium-length muzzle, dark beard and moustache, and a very long coat, which drapes to the ground. Colours include, gold, cream, honey, grey, brown and black and white. The ears are heavily feathered, and the tail is carried over the back

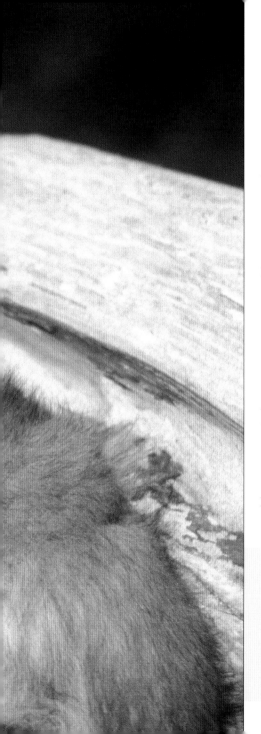

SHIH TZU

Similar in appearance to both the Pekingese and the Tibetan Lhasa Apso, it is thought that the Shih Tzu may have resulted from crossbreeding between these two breeds, which were often traded as gifts between the Chinese Emperor and the Dalai Lama, and all are sometimes known as 'lion dogs', referring to the mythical animal of Chinese legend that was half lion and half dog. The lion is also greatly revered in Buddhism, and these little dogs were held sacred as monastery guardians and as companions at the Imperial Chinese courts. As with the Lhasa Apso, the sale of the Shih Tzu was forbidden, and as foreigners were largely unwelcome in China for many years, this dog remained unknown to the West for perhaps centuries, first being introduced to Britain during the 1930s. Since that time, this lively, intelligent and attractive breed has become highly popular as a companion and show dog.

HEIGHT: 20–28cm (8–11in)
WEIGHT: 4–7kg (9–16lb)
LIFE EXPECTANCY: 14–16 years
ORIGIN: China
DESCRIPTION: A small but sturdy dog, with a short muzzle, profuse beard and moustache, small pendant ears, and a tail that is carried curled over the back. The coat is long and dense, and colours include, gold white, black and grey

TIBETAN SPANIEL

HEIGHT: 23–25cm (9–10in)
WEIGHT: 4–7kg (9–15lb)
LIFE EXPECTANCY: 13–15 years
ORIGIN: Tibet
DESCRIPTION: A small, slightly elongated dog, with a relatively small head and blunt, medium-length muzzle. The ears are high-set and pendant, and the plumed tail curls over its back. The medium-length coat may be fawn, red, black, white or black and tan

Although the Tibetan Spaniel may be related to the Japanese Chin, which is sometimes also known as the Japanese Spaniel, this breed is not closely related to the more familiar European spaniels, but rather, is thought to share a common ancestry with such breeds as the Pekingese, Lhasa Apso and Shih Tzu, and like those dogs, it is sometimes referred to as a 'lion dog': an animal revered in several Eastern cultures. The Tibetan Spaniel was common in Tibetan monasteries, where it was employed as a watchdog, and also given the task of turning the prayer wheels by means of a treadmill, which has led to its alternative name of Prayer Dog. As with its close relations, it was often traded as a gift, particularly with visiting Chinese dignitaries, but it was not introduced to the West until the late 1800s, and not in any great numbers until the 1940s. Since that time however, this lively and affectionate dog has become increasingly popular as both a companion and show dog.

TIBETAN TERRIER

Like the closely related Lhasa Apso, this breed looks more like a miniature Old English Sheepdog than a true terrier, and in fact, was originally employed for guarding and herding livestock, as well as being found in Tibetan monasteries as a guard and companion. It is thought to be the original sacred dog of Tibet, and to have contributed to the development of the Lhasa Apso, Tibetan Spaniel and Shih Tzu amongst others, and like those dogs, it was not widely known outside its native country for many years. The breed was introduced to the West primarily by a Mrs Greig during the 1920s, who was first given a Tibetan Terrier as a gift after treating a sick Tibetan patient, and would later establish a breeding kennels in England to promote the breed. Hardy, intelligent and affectionate, but typically reserved with strangers, the Tibetan Terrier makes an excellent companion and watchdog, which also often excels at competitive agility and obedience trials.

HEIGHT: 36–43cm (14–17in)
WEIGHT: 8–14kg (18–30lb)
LIFE EXPECTANCY: 12–14 years
ORIGIN: Tibet
DESCRIPTION: A medium-sized, muscular dog, with a long, profuse coat, which may be straight or wavy, and occurs in a wide variety of colours and combinations. The tail is carried over the back, whilst the ears are pendant, and both are well-feathered

CHIHUAHUA

Named after the Mexican province where it is thought that it may have originated, the Chihuahua is amongst the oldest breeds developed in the Americas and the smallest dog in the world. Its ancestry is believed to date back to an ancient breed, known to the Mayans as the Techichi, the descendants of which may have later been crossed with hairless dogs of Mexican or Asian origin, or other small dogs native to Central and South America. Occurring in both a long- and short-coated form, it is possible that the long-haired variety was subsequently developed by the further introduction of Pomeranian, Papillon and Yorkshire Terrier blood. A popular companion dog, the Chihuahua is intelligent, affectionate and loyal, but it is typically aggressive towards other breeds, can be snappy with strangers, and may be susceptible to injury and cold temperatures on account of its size. If it remains healthy, however, it is usually a long-lived breed.

HEIGHT: 15–23cm (6–9in)
WEIGHT: 1–3kg (2–6lb)
LIFE EXPECTANCY: 13–15 years
ORIGIN: Mexico
DESCRIPTION: A very small dog, with a rounded head and short but pointed muzzle. The eyes and ears are large, the tail quite long and often carried curled over the back. The coat may be long or short, and colours include sandy, fawn, chestnut, grey-blue and black and tan

CAVALIER KING CHARLES SPANIEL

HEIGHT: 30–33cm (12–13in)
WEIGHT: 5–8kg (10–18lb)
LIFE EXPECTANCY: 12–14 years
ORIGIN: Britain
DESCRIPTION: A small spaniel, with a long, silky coat, fairly flat skull and conical muzzle. The ears are long and feathered, as is the tail, although this is sometimes docked. The coat may be ruby, black and tan with or without white, and chestnut and white

Toy spaniels were particularly popular in the royal courts of England during the 16th, 17th and 18th centuries, and were given the title King Charles Spaniels after King Charles II, during the reign of the Stuarts. Then, during the 18th and 19th centuries, following the development of the chestnut and white or 'Blenheim' colour, the type began to be standardized, giving rise to the rather flat-faced, domed-skulled dogs, that we know as the King Charles Spaniel today. However, as a reaction to this, certain breeders, notably an American named Mr Roswell Eldridge, attempted to recreate the larger, longer-nosed, flat-skulled variety, that he perceived as being closer in appearance to the original toy spaniels, as depicted in paintings by such artists as Titian, Van Dyck, Stubbs, Reynolds and Gainsborough. This was something of a slow process, but by the 1940s the two types were recognized as distinct breeds, and the prefix 'Cavalier' was introduced to distinguish them.

JAPANESE CHIN

With its profuse, silky coat, plumed tail and rather flattened face, the Japanese Chin is reminiscent of the Pekingese of China. However, it is longer-legged and more slightly built than that breed with a more spaniel-like appearance. It is sometimes known as the Japanese Spaniel, although it is actually thought to have originated in an earlier form in Korea. Essentially a companion breed, the Japanese Chin was bred as a lapdog for the Japanese aristocracy, and was a favourite of the imperial courts, before being introduced to the West around 1700. There too it became popular with royalty, and in 1853 two of these dogs were presented as a gift to Queen Victoria. An affectionate and devoted pet, the Japanese Chin is highly playful, yet relatively easy to train, and it often excels at learning and performing tricks.

HEIGHT: 18–28cm (7–11in)
WEIGHT: 2–3kg (4–7lb)
LIFE EXPECTANCY: 8–10 years
ORIGIN: Japan
DESCRIPTION: A lightly built dog, with a broad face, large eyes and upturned muzzle. The coat is well-feathered, with a dense ruff around the neck and chest, long hair on the ears, and a plumed tail that curls over the back. Colours include white with black, red, yellow or tan patches

PEKINGESE

An ancient breed, which originated in Imperial China, the Pekingese is regarded as one of the 'lion dogs', which were once widely held as sacred in the East, and for hundreds of years, only the Emperors, their families and courtiers were permitted to own them, and so the breed remained largely unknown to the outside world. Some examples began to appear in the West during the 17th century, but it was not until 1860 when British and French troops stormed the Summer Palace that some of the foundation stock for the breed as we know it today, was stolen and taken to Britain. Queen Victoria is known to have been presented with one of these dogs, which she appropriately named 'Looty'. The Pekingese was first shown in England in 1893, and recognized by the British Kennel Club five years later. Since that time, this rather distinctive and endearing breed has become a popular companion and show dog around the world.

HEIGHT: 15–23cm (6–9in)
WEIGHT: 3–6kg (7–12lb)
LIFE EXPECTANCY: 12–14 years
ORIGIN: China
DESCRIPTION: A small, short-legged dog, with a Pug-like face, long, pendant, well-feathered ears, and a high-set, plumed tail, which is carried curled over to one side. The coat is long and dense, and occurs in a very large range of colours

FRENCH BULLDOG

HEIGHT: 28–33cm
   (11–13in)
WEIGHT: 10–13kg
   (22–28lb)
LIFE EXPECTANCY: 10–12
   years
ORIGIN: France
DESCRIPTION: A small,
   compact bulldog with
   erect, bat-like ears. The
   face is pug-like, with an
   undershot muzzle. The
   coat is short and soft,
   and may be brindle,
   fawn, white or
   combinations of those
   colours. The tail may be
   straight or cork-screwed

During the mid-19th century, miniature or toy English
Bulldogs became popular as companion or lapdogs,
particularly amongst female workers who were involved
in the lace-making industries. When many of these
workers moved to France in search of better pay, they
often took their dogs with them, where they are thought
to have been crossbred with French terriers, resulting in
the first French Bulldogs. Like its larger counterpart, the
French Bulldog is a compact and muscular dog, with a
large square head. Its most distinctive is its erect, bat-like
ears. Although it may sometimes be wilful, the French
Bulldog is affectionate and playful, and thrives on human
companionship, making it an amiable, amusing and easily
cared for pet. However, like other bulldog breeds, it can
be susceptible to respiratory problems, particularly in
hot weather.

PUG

A distinctive little dog of Chinese origin, the Pug is thought to have first been introduced to the West by Portuguese traders during the 1500s. It became particularly popular in Holland, where it was the official dog of the House of Orange, before becoming fashionable in many of the royal courts of Europe. Napoleon's wife, Josephine was known to have owned a pug, as were Henry II of France, Marie Antoinette, the artist William Hogarth and William III and Queen Mary, who are believed to have first brought the Pug to Britain. However, it reached its peak of popularity during the reign of Queen Victoria, and has been owned by people from all walks of life. Loyal, affectionate and playful, the Pug remains a popular companion to this day, and being quick to learn, it is often also seen as a performing dog.

HEIGHT: 25–30cm (10–12in)
WEIGHT: 6–9kg (13–20lb)
LIFE EXPECTANCY: 12–14 years
ORIGIN: China
DESCRIPTION: A compact, dog with a short, flat, dark muzzle, velvety ears and prominent eyes. The tail is usually carried in a tight curl. Coat colours include silver or apricot fawn with a black mask, and black overall

BOSTON TERRIER

Considered by many to be the national dog of the USA, the Boston Terrier is named after the city where it first originated in 1865, as the result of crossbreeding between the now extinct English White Terrier and an English Bulldog, and this breed is still sometimes known as the Boston Bull. Initially developed as a much larger, fighting dog, it was gradually bred to be smaller and less aggressive, and after dog fighting was banned, found favour as both a ratter and a companion dog. Intelligent, affectionate and relatively easy to train, today it remains a popular family pet, particularly in America. The Boston Terrier is generally easy to care for and usually quite long-lived, but it can experience breathing difficulties in very hot and cold weather, or if overexerted, and may also snore and drool. Giving birth can also be difficult for this breed, on account of the broad heads of the pups, and delivery by caesarean section is often necessary.

Height: 38–43cm (15–17in)
Weight: 5–11kg (10–25lb)
Life expectancy: 12–14 years
Origin: USA
Description: A small, compact, but muscular terrier, with a distinctive short square muzzle, short tail, erect ears and prominent, bulging eyes. The coat is short and colours include brindle, black or brown, with white markings

INDEX

PICTURE ACKNOWLEDGMENTS

The publisher would like to thank Photolibrary.com and Ardea.com for providing the photographs in this book. We would also like to thank the following for their kind permission to reproduce their photographs.

Ausloos, Henry 5,9,26,39,40,138,158,207,227   Bender, Richard 50   Bender, Rolf 180   Bph, Fotograpfie 59   Brinkmann, Bernd 3,7,10,115,120,122,206,252   Carey, Alan & Sandy 36,58,80,204   Conte, Margot 56,83   Daniels, John 6,22,33,38,52,77,78,82,88,96,99,100,102,123,140,146,152,159,164,165,176, 178,184,186,189,194,195,198,202,203,231,234,235,246,250   De Meester, Johan 179,188,228 DK Ltd 160   Enger, Don 104,114   Ertiet, Cheryl A/OKAPIA 135,200   Ferrero, J.P 55, 175,193, 199   Gardiner, Pammy 134,248   Hamblin, Mark 15,20,24,48,116,117,136,212   Harrison, Jeannie 74   Klein, JL & Hubert, ML 14, 32, 46, 49, 51, 71, 101,156,188,208,225,226,220,244   Kolar, Richard/AA 132   Labat, J-M 110   Leszczynski, Zig/AA 63,64,90,183,251   Lockwood, C.C 236   Marchington, James 147   Mauritus die Bildagentur Gmbh 34, 174,211   Meier, Bruno 196   O' Dell, Lynn 150   Okapia 243   Osf 28   Pearcy, Eunice 62, 111,168,214,216,230,247   Pearcy, Robert 35,66,70,76,93,98,103,129,142,144,148,151,153,190,224,240,237   Reed, Michael & Barbara/AA 17,218   Reinhard, Hans 30,54,171   Reinhold, Ralph 8,44,67,84,106,108,112,128,130,157,162,166,170,172, 176, 182,222, 232   Rosing, Norbert 92   Smith, Nigel/AA 43   Steuwer, Sabine 126   Thompson, Sydney 127   Tipling, David 18 ,124   Tull, Philip 154   Valla, Daniel/SAL 86   Vock, KG 60   Von Hoffman, Barbara 192,210,217,238   Weinmann, Peter 42,141   Wothe, Konrad 89   Wright, Barbara 68   Yann Arthus Bertrand 72

Front cover image: Mark Hamblin
Back cover image: Bernd Brinkmann
Back flap image: Ian West